THE GUT REPAIR
COOKBOOK

*Transform Your Health with 130+ Delicious
and Easy, Gut-Healing Recipes*

DR. JOSH AXE

Published in 2016 by Axe Wellness LLC
Copyright © 2016 Dr. Josh Axe
All rights reserved

Visit our website at www.draxe.com.

ISBN-13: 978-0-692-64685-4

Photography and design: Jessica Heggan, Ayla Sadler and Allison Brochey

Printed in the USA

contents

Dr. Josh Axe

About Dr. Josh Axe

Josh Axe, DNM, DC, CNS, is a doctor of natural medicine, nutritionist and author with a passion to help people get well using food as medicine and operates one of the world's largest natural health websites at www.DrAxe.com. He's the author of the recent smash-hit book *Eat Dirt* (a book all about gut health) and *The Real Food Diet Cookbook*, and co-author of *Essential Oils: Ancient Medicine for a Modern World*.

Dr. Axe has been a physician for many professional athletes. In 2009, he began working with the Wellness Advisory Council and traveled to the 2012 Games in London to work with USA athletes. Dr. Axe is an expert in herbal medicine, digestive health and athletic performance. He has been featured on many television shows and stations, including The Dr. Oz Show, CBS and NBC. In 2008, he started

Exodus Health Center, which grew to become one of the largest natural health care clinics in the world.

At his website, DrAxe.com, the main topics covered include nutrition, natural medicine for various health conditions, fitness, healthy recipes, DIY home remedies and trending health news. In addition, Dr. Axe puts out popular digital programs that include webinars, videos, podcasts, Q&As and ebooks. Dr. Axe also released several supplement lines, including Ancient Nutrition (featuring bone broth protein and collagen powders) and Axe Organics.

In his spare time, Dr. Axe competes in triathlons and does "Burst" training with his wife Chelsea, who is also a health enthusiast.

Who Needs the
Gut Repair Cookbook?
(Everyone!)

As I discuss extensively in my book *Eat Dirt: Why Leaky Gut May Be the Root Cause of Your Health Problems and 5 Surprising Steps to Cure it* (Harper Wave, 2016), a healthy gut almost always results in a healthy you. Unfortunately, though, most of us are walking around with a damaged digestive system.

In fact, a damaged gut is the root cause of all disease. Hippocrates, the father of modern medicine, said that "all disease begins in the gut." (Similarly, all health begins in the gut as well.) The cause of everything from your food allergies, low energy and slow metabolism to your joint pain, thyroid disease and even autoimmune conditions could be your damaged gut.

Think of the lining of your digestive tract like a net with extremely small holes in it that only allow specific substances to pass through. Your gut lining works as a barrier keeping out bigger particles that can damage your system. With a damaged gut, the "net" in your digestive tract gets damaged, which causes even bigger holes to develop in it, so things that normally can't pass through are now be able to.

Some of the things that can now pass through include gluten, bad bacteria and undigested foods particles. Toxic waste can also leak from the inside of your intestinal wall into your bloodstream and cause inflammation and an immune reaction.

One of the biggest warning signs that you have a damaged gut? Multiple food sensitivities, which may not manifest in a rash necessarily but instead can trigger certain symptoms that, if left unaddressed, can usher in more severe health issues.

Curious if you have a damaged gut? Get a "gut rank health score" by taking my free quiz at: www.isyourgutleaking.com

The Importance of the
MICROBIOME
by the Numbers

90%
Up to 90% of all disease can be traced in some way back to the gut and health of the microbiome

10–100 trillion
Number of symbiotic microbial cells harbored by each person, primarily bacteria in the gut, that make up the human microbiota

>10,000
Number of different microbe species researchers have identified living in the human body

10X
There are 10 times as many outside organisms as there are human cells in the human body

100

100 to 1
The genes in our microbiome outnumber the genes in our genome by about 100 to 1

22,000
Approximate number of genes in the human gene catalog

3.3 million
Number of non-redundant genes in the human gut microbiome

99.9%

Percentage of individual humans that are identical to one another in terms of host genome

Percentage of individual humans that are different from one another in terms of the microbiome

80%–90%

What causes a damaged gut exactly? There are four principle causes: poor diet, chronic stress, toxin overload and bacterial imbalance.

Diet-wise, the most common components of food that can damage your intestinal lining are the proteins found in un-sprouted grains, sugar, genetically modified organisms (GMOs) and conventional dairy.

The problem with un-sprouted grains is that they contain large amounts of antinutrients or nutrient blockers called phytates and lectins, which damage your gut and cause inflammation. Sugar feeds the growth of yeast, candida and bad bacteria, which will further damage your gut. GMOs increase your allergies and antibiotic resistance while causing problems with your endocrine system as well as your reproductive system. It's never been more important to eat whole foods and support your local farmers market!

Regarding conventional dairy, the component that will damage your gut is the protein A1 casein. Also, the pasteurization process will destroy vital enzymes, making sugars like lactose very difficult to digest.

Next, the reality is that chronic stress and toxin overload are very hard to dismiss entirely in our modern lives. Chronic stress can weaken your immune system over time and cripple your ability to fight off foreign invaders like bad bacteria and viruses, leading to inflammation and a damaged gut.

Regarding toxins, we come into contact with over 80,000 (!) chemicals and toxins every single year. The worst offenders for causing a damaged gut include antibiotics, pesticides, tap water, aspirin and nonsteroidal anti-inflammatory drugs (like ibuprofen).

Guess what? This toxin overload directly causes bacterial imbalance. The great news is that we can reverse course quickly. By bringing back the right foods and habits, we can also welcome the return of our beneficial microbes.

The path to healing your damaged gut is straightforward: 1) Remove the foods and factors that damage the gut; 2) replace and rebalance with certain healing and probiotic foods.

This cookbook represents the easiest way for you to take steps 1 and 2, as you won't find any gut-damaging ingredients in any of my recipes. Instead, each dish uses the most gut-healing foods that exist (more on that next).

Gut Repair Starts
with the Right Foods

While a poor diet plays a big role in creating poor gut health, luckily, the converse is true as well. Yes, consuming the right foods can reverse your poor gut health and support your microbiome's good bacteria — and it's why I created this cookbook.

In fact, research over the past several decades has revealed that there's an inextricable link between a person's microbiota, digestion, body weight and metabolism. In an analysis of humans and 59 additional mammalian species, microbiome environments were shown to differ dramatically depending on the species' diet.

For example, gut microbiota play an important role in obesity, and changes in bacterial strains in the gut have been shown to lead to significant changes in health and body weight after only a few days. In a study published by the National Academy of Sciences, when lean, germ-free mice received a transplant of gut microbiota from conventional/fat mice, they acquired more body fat quickly without even increasing food intake. Why? Their gut bugs directly influenced hormone production (like insulin), nutrient extraction and fat storage.

So what are the best diet steps to take and the best foods eat in order to begin improving your gut health today?

One of the first crucial steps is to focus on consuming foods that are grown locally. The microbes found in your local soil on that piece of carrot or lettuce will actually help you better digest the foods grown in your area, while also providing your body with a customized immune defense to pathogens you may be exposed to regularly. The best route to good health is to get these microbes in small doses over time — a little bit every day.

Next, before discussing the foods you want to get into your diet pronto, you must know which foods to start avoiding. These include all grains, especially ones that contain gluten like wheat, as gluten–containing grains can damage your intestinal lining and cause leaky gut syndrome.

Once your gut is healthy, you can occasionally eat grains that have been fermented and sprouted. Sprouting and fermenting grains reduces phytates and lectins, making these foods easier to digest. GMO and hybridized foods tend to be the highest in lectins since they have been modified to fight off bugs, so avoid these like the plague.

Conventional cow's milk is another food that can harm your gut. The component of dairy that will damage your gut is the protein A1 casein. Also, the pasteurization process will destroy vital enzymes, making sugars like lactose very difficult to digest. For this reason, I only recommend buying dairy that is raw and from A2 cows, goats, sheep or even buffalo.

Then there's sugar, yet another substance that will wreak havoc on your digestive system. Sugar feeds the growth of yeast, candida and bad bacteria, which will further damage your gut. Bad bacteria actually creates toxins called exotoxins that damage healthy cells and can eat holes into your intestinal wall.

Instead of those gut-damaging foods, you'll see plenty of the following gut-healing foods in this book's recipes.

That list must begin with bone broth, which contains collagen and the amino acids proline and glycine that can help heal your damaged cell walls. In fact, I've had many patients do a bone broth fast for three days to address a severely damaged gut. (For some people, regularly making bone broth

and getting access to collagen is challenging. For those, I recommend looking into bone broth and collagen supplements.)

Rather than conventional dairy, I recommend raw cultured dairy, which contains both probiotics and short-chain fatty acids that can help heal the gut. Pastured kefir, yogurt, amasai, butter, ghee and raw cheese are some of the best.

Fermented vegetables are also key, for they contain organic acids that balance intestinal pH and probiotics to support the gut. Sauerkraut, kimchi and kvass are excellent sources.

With coconuts, it's easy. All coconut products are especially good for your gut, as its medium-chain fatty acids are easier to digest. Also, coconut kefir contains probiotics that support your digestive system.

Sprouted seeds like chia seeds, flaxseeds and hemp seeds are great sources of fiber that can help support the growth of beneficial bacteria. But if you have a highly sensitive, damaged gut, you may need to start out getting your fiber from steamed vegetables and fruit first. (See my suggested "Gut Repair 7-Day Meal Plan" on pages 16 and 17.)

Speaking of fruit, consuming 1 to 2 servings of fruit daily is good on a damaged gut diet — but not necessarily raw fruit. Instead, you can steam apples and pears to make homemade applesauce or fruit sauce. Overall, fruit is best consumed in the morning and not later in the day.

For vegetables, you're looking at 4 to 5 servings per day, including cruciferous vegetables (broccoli, cabbage, cauliflower); dark, leafy greens (collard greens, kale, spinach); sea vegetables; and squashes, sweet potatoes and carrots — all cooked.

When it comes to protein foods, it's important to consume the ones that also have anti-inflammatory omega-3 fats, such as grass-fed beef, bison, lamb and wild-caught fish like salmon.

While grains should be kept to a bare minimum, some ancient grains and legumes/beans may be consumed. They're best when sprouted and 100 percent unrefined/whole. Sources include Anasazi beans, adzuki beans, black beans, black-eyed peas, chickpeas, lentils, black rice, amaranth, buckwheat and quinoa.

Of course, it's also important to have flavor in your foods and drinks. So you'll see gut-friendly herbs and spices throughout this cookbook — including turmeric, ginger, basil, oregano and thyme, plus certain teas in moderation. Plus, here's an additional perk: You may consume red wine and dark chocolate/cocoa in moderation, and you'll see many desserts that are not only good for your gut but also filling and delicious.

Time to get cooking, in a new, gut-restoring way!

Gut-Repairing Foods

Bone Broth
made from organic free-range chicken, grass-fed beef or wild-caught fish

Kefir and fermented dairy
goat, A2 cows, sheep or buffalo milk and raw (unpasteurized)

Cooked vegetables
cruciferous veggies, leafy greens, carrots, sweet potatoes, squash, Brussels sprouts, etc.

Fermented vegetables
sauerkraut, kimchi, pickled veggies

Omega-3 and protein-rich foods
wild salmon, grass-fed beef, and free-range chicken and eggs

Herbs, spices and teas
turmeric, ginger, basil, chai, green tea

Healthy fats
coconut oil (and other coconut products), ghee, MCT oil, avocados

Select fruits
blueberries, cherries, nectarines, plums

Gut-Damaging Foods

Refined vegetable oils
canola, corn, soybean

**Refined carbohydrates and
processed grain products**

**Pasteurized dairy
products**

**Conventional meat,
poultry and eggs**

**Trans fats/
hydrogenated fats**
packaged/processed
products, fried foods

Added sugars
packaged snacks, breads,
condiments, canned items, cereals

GUT REPAIR 7-Day Meal Plan

	MONDAY	TUESDAY	WEDNESDAY
BREAKFAST	Cherry Vanilla Collagen Smoothie*	Roasted Peaches with Kefir and Raw Honey Turmeric Tea	Blueberry Bliss Collagen Smoothie*
LUNCH	Chicken Ginger Lemongrass Soup	French Onion Soup	Chicken Teriyaki Soup
SNACK	Glass of bone broth**	No-Bake Bone Broth Protein Bar	Sweet Potato Hummus, served with steamed vegetables
DINNER	Shepherd's Pie	Zucchini Noodle Nourish Bowl with Chicken and Vegetables	Lamb Stuffed Cabbage Rolls Baked Cauliflower

* Use collagen protein or bone broth protein interchangeably.
** Use the homemade bone broth recipes from this book or bone broth protein powder with water.

THURSDAY	FRIDAY	SATURDAY	SUNDAY
Egg Scramble with Kale, Garlic and Onions Chai Tea	Chocolate Bone Broth Protein Shake*	Sweet Potato Pancakes Turmeric Tea	Cauliflower Mushroom Kale Frittata Chai Tea
Carrot Fennel Soup Grilled Asparagus	Acorn Squash Bisque Coconut Crusted Chicken Tenders	Chicken "Zoodle" Soup	Salmon Cakes Potato Leek Soup
Spinach and Goat Cheese Stuffed Mushrooms	Glass of bone broth**	Blueberry Broth Bar	Guacamole Apple Chips
Chicken Pot Pie	Seared Ahi Tuna Stir-Fry Cauliflower Rice	Paleo Meatloaf Braised Cabbage	Chicken Marsala Sautéed Spinach with Garlic

CHAPTER 1

Breakfasts and Beverages

TURMERIC TEA

Serving Size: 2   **Time: 5 minutes**

- **1 cup full-fat coconut milk**
- **1 cup water**
- **1 tablespoon ghee**
- **1 tablespoon raw honey**
- **1 teaspoon turmeric (powder or grated root)**

1. Pour the coconut milk and water into a saucepan and warm for 2 minutes.
2. Add in the ghee, raw honey and turmeric powder for another 2 minutes.
3. Stir and pour into glasses.

CARROT GINGER CHICKEN BROTH SHAKE

Serving Size: 2   **Time: 5 minutes**

- **3 cups grated carrots**
- **1-inch piece fresh ginger, peeled and chopped**
- **3 tablespoons bone broth protein powder**
- **1¼ cup full-fat coconut milk**
- **1 tablespoon raw honey**
- **Handful of ice cubes**

1. Place all ingredients in a high-speed blender and purée until smooth. Serve immediately.

CHERRY VANILLA COLLAGEN SMOOTHIE

Serving Size: 1   Time: 5 minutes

- 1 cup full-fat coconut milk
- 2 teaspoons coconut oil, melted
- 1 cup frozen cherries
- 2 tablespoons collagen protein powder
- 2–3 Medjool dates, pitted
- 3–4 ice cubes

1. Place all of the ingredients in a high-speed blender and purée until smooth, adding more coconut milk to blend as necessary.

CHOCOLATE BONE BROTH PROTEIN SHAKE

Serving Size: 1   Time: 5 minutes

- 1 cup full-fat coconut milk
- ¼ avocado
- 1 tablespoon cacao powder
- 2 tablespoons chocolate bone broth protein powder
- 1 teaspoon chia seeds
- Handful of ice cubes
- 2–3 drops liquid stevia (optional)

1. Place all ingredients in a high-speed blender and purée until smooth, adding more coconut milk to blend as necessary.

CAULIFLOWER MUSHROOM KALE FRITTATA

Serving Size: 6   Time: 55 minutes

- 1 medium head of cauliflower, chopped
- 2 cups chopped mushrooms
- 3 cups chopped kale, stems removed
- 1 tablespoon coconut oil, melted
- 2 teaspoons sea salt
- 2 tablespoons black pepper
- 10 eggs
- Sea salt and pepper to taste

1. Heat the oven to 400 F.
2. Grease a medium cast iron skillet with coconut oil. In the cast iron, toss the cauliflower, mushrooms and kale with the melted coconut oil, salt and pepper until well coated.
3. Whisk the eggs in a medium mixing bowl. Pour the eggs over the vegetables and season with salt and pepper to taste.
4. Bake the frittata for 50–55 minutes, or until the top is golden and set.
5. Remove the frittata from the oven.
6. Allow to cool for 5–10 minutes before serving.

CHAI TEA

Serving Size: 1   Time: 5 minutes

- 1 cup full-fat coconut milk
- 1 tablespoon maple syrup
- Sprinkles of nutmeg, cinnamon and clove

1. Mix all ingredients in a small saucepan and cook over medium heat until warm.

BISON HASH

WITH PEPPERS, KALE AND ASPARAGUS

Serving Size: 4   Time: 20 minutes

- **1 pound ground bison**
- **2 cups chopped asparagus**
- **1 red bell pepper, diced**
- **2 cups chopped kale, stems removed**
- **2 large garlic cloves, chopped**
- **1 teaspoon sea salt**
- **1 teaspoon black pepper**

1. Heat the skillet to medium-high heat and add the ground bison, using a spatula to break up the meat.
2. Remove the bottom two inches of the asparagus and chop the remainder into 1-inch pieces.
3. Once the meat is broken up and almost cooked through, add the asparagus, bell pepper, kale, garlic, salt and pepper, and sauté for about 8 minutes, or until the vegetables are tender.
4. Take the skillet off the heat and serve immediately.

EGG SCRAMBLE

WITH KALE, GARLIC AND ONIONS

Serving Size: 1–2   Time: 15 minutes

- **2 teaspoons coconut oil**
- **1 cup chopped kale, stems removed**
- **1 garlic clove, minced**
- **¼ cup diced red onion**
- **4 egg yolks**
- **2 tablespoons water**
- **1 teaspoon each: sea salt and black pepper**

1. Heat a skillet to medium heat and add the coconut oil. Once the oil is hot, add the kale, garlic and onion and sauté for 2–3 minutes, or until the onions pieces are softened.
2. Whisk together the egg yolks, water, salt and pepper in a small bowl and add the mixture to the skillet.
3. Let the eggs cook for 1 minute, and then use a spatula to scramble the mixture.
4. Divide the scramble between two plates and eat immediately.

Bison Hash

Strawberry Coconut Bone Broth Smoothie

STRAWBERRY COCONUT BONE BROTH SMOOTHIE

Serving Size: 4   Time: 5 minutes

- ¾ cup full-fat coconut milk
- 1 tablespoon bone broth powder (pure or vanilla)
- 3 cups strawberries
- ½ tablespoon vanilla extract
- 1 tablespoon raw honey
- 1 cup ice

1. Place all ingredients in a high-speed blender and purée until smooth, adding more coconut milk to blend as necessary.

BLUEBERRY BLISS COLLAGEN SMOOTHIE

Serving Size: 2   Time: 5 minutes

- 1½ cups fresh or frozen blueberries
- 5 macadamia nuts
- 1 teaspoon vanilla extract
- 1 tablespoon raw honey or 2–3 drops liquid stevia (optional)
- 2 tablespoons collagen protein powder
- 2 cups full-fat coconut milk

1. Place all ingredients in a high-speed blender and purée until smooth, adding more coconut milk to blend as necessary.

ROASTED PEACHES
WITH KEFIR AND RAW HONEY

Serving Size: 4   Time: 1 hour 20 minutes

- **1 cup kefir**
- **3 tablespoons raw honey**
- **1 tablespoon chia seeds**
- **Juice of 1 lemon**
- **One 2-inch piece fresh ginger, peeled and grated**
- **6 ripe peaches, pitted and quartered**

1. Preheat the oven to 350 F.
2. Combine the kefir, honey and chia seeds in a small bowl. Cover and refrigerate.
3. Stir together the lemon juice and ginger in a medium bowl. Toss the peaches in the mixture and coat evenly.
4. Arrange the peaches on a baking sheet lined with parchment paper.
5. Bake for 15 minutes.
6. Remove from the oven and serve with the kefir and raw honey mixture.

CHOCOLATE RASPBERRY COLLAGEN SHAKE

Serving Size: 1   Time: 5 minutes

- **1 cup full-fat coconut milk**
- **1 cup frozen raspberries**
- **¼ avocado**
- **1 tablespoon cacao powder**
- **2 tablespoons collagen protein powder**
- **2–3 drops stevia (optional)**
- **3–4 ice cubes**

1. Place all ingredients in a high-speed blender and purée until smooth, adding more coconut milk to blend as necessary.

SWEET POTATO PANCAKES

Serving Size: 4   Time: 45 minutes

- **1 tablespoon coconut oil**
- **2 medium sweet potatoes**
- **4 eggs**
- **¾ cup almond flour**
- **½ cup coconut flour**
- **¼ cup full-fat coconut milk, plus additional as needed**
- **2 teaspoons vanilla extract**
- **1½ teaspoon cinnamon**
- **1 teaspoon ground ginger**

1. Preheat the oven to 375 F. Grease a baking sheet with the coconut oil. Cut the sweet potatoes in half, lengthwise, and place face down on the sheet.
2. Bake for 30 minutes, or until fork tender. Allow the sweet potatoes to cool before removing the skin.
3. Add the potato flesh along with all other ingredients in a high-speed blender and blend on high until well combined.
4. Heat a pan over medium-low heat and coat with coconut oil. Pour ¼ cup of the batter to form each pancake. Cook for a few minutes. Once it starts to bubble on top, flip and cook an additional 1-2 minutes. Plate and serve.

EGG SCRAMBLE

WITH ASPARAGUS, AVOCADO AND KRAUT

Serving Size: 1–2   Time: 10 minutes

- 2 teaspoons coconut oil
- 1 cup chopped asparagus
- 4 egg yolks
- 2 tablespoons water
- ½ teaspoon sea salt
- ¼ teaspoon black pepper
- ½ avocado, peeled and sliced
- ¼ cup sauerkraut

1. Heat a skillet to medium heat and add the coconut oil. Once the oil is hot, add the chopped asparagus and sauté for 2–3 minutes, or until the asparagus is slightly softened.
2. Whisk together the egg yolks, water, salt and pepper in a medium bowl, and add the mixture to the asparagus.
3. Let the eggs cook for 1 minute, and then use a spatula to scramble the mixture.
4. Scoop the egg scramble onto a plate and top with the avocado and sauerkraut.

ALMOND/CASHEW MILK

Serving Size: 6–8   Time: 20 minutes

- **1 cup raw, unsalted almonds (or cashews)**
- **2 cups water, plus additional for soaking**
- **Liquid stevia to taste**

1. Place 1 cup of almonds (or cashews) in a glass bowl and add enough water to cover them.
2. Soak the almonds in water for 24 to 48 hours.
3. After 24 to 48 hours, drain and rinse the almonds.
4. Next, add the almonds and 2 cups of water together in a high-speed blender.
5. Blend for 2 minutes.
6. Using a cheesecloth, strain out the almonds.
7. Press out the almond milk from meal (through the cheesecloth).
8. Sweeten with the liquid stevia, to taste.

MAPLE BREAKFAST SAUSAGE

Serving Size: 4   Time: 25 minutes

- **1 pound grass-fed ground beef**
- **2 tablespoons coconut aminos**
- **½ cup maple syrup**
- **2 tablespoons ghee**

1. Mix the ground beef, coconut aminos and maple syrup together in a large bowl.
2. Place a frying pan over low heat and add the ghee.
3. Form the meat into sausage links and place them in the pan.
4. Cook with the lid on for 15–20 minutes, or until cooked through.

GINGERED BAKED APPLES
WITH GOAT MILK YOGURT AND RAW HONEY

Serving Size: 6   Time: 35 minutes

- **1 cup goat milk yogurt**
- **3 tablespoons raw honey**
- **6 ripe Gala apples, cored and chopped**
- **Juice of 1 lemon**
- **One 2-inch piece of fresh ginger, peeled and minced**

1. Preheat the oven to 375 F.
2. Combine the yogurt and honey in a small bowl. Mix well, cover and refrigerate.
3. Arrange the apples in an 8 x 8 baking dish.
4. Stir together the lemon juice and ginger in a medium bowl. Pour the mixture over the apples, coating evenly.
5. Bake for 30 minutes, stirring occasionally.
6. Remove from the oven and serve over the yogurt and raw honey mixture.

Maple Breakfast Sausage

Ghee Waffles

GHEE WAFFLES

Serving Size: 4   **Time: 15 minutes**

- **2 eggs**
- **½ cup ghee, melted**
- **¼–½ cup full-fat coconut milk**
- **1½–2 cups almond flour**
- **1 tablespoon coconut flour**
- **1 tablespoon raw honey**
- **1 teaspoon baking powder**
- **½ teaspoon cinnamon**
- **¼ teaspoon sea salt**
- **1 teaspoon vanilla extract**

1. Beat the eggs until fluffy in a medium bowl.
2. Mix in the melted ghee and coconut milk.
3. Add the almond flour, coconut flour, honey, baking powder, cinnamon, salt and vanilla until just combined.
4. Lightly oil a preheated waffle iron. Pour ½–¾ cup of the mixture into the waffle iron and cook until golden brown.

TURKEY BREAKFAST SAUSAGE

Serving Size: 4   **Time: 20 minutes**

- **½ small onion, finely diced**
- **2 tablespoons unsalted grass-fed butter (divided)**
- **1 pound ground turkey**
- **¼ teaspoon each: cumin, marjoram, black pepper, oregano, cayenne pepper and ginger**
- **½ teaspoon each: basil, thyme and sage**
- **2 teaspoons sea salt**
- **2 tablespoons almond flour**
- **1 egg, lightly beaten**

1. Sauté the onion in 1 tablespoon of the butter in a medium-sized pan until soft and translucent.
2. Combine rest of ingredients (except remaining butter) in a large bowl. Form into patties.
3. Melt the remaining butter in the pan, then add the patties and cook for several minutes on each side until done.

FRITTATA

WITH ZUCCHINI, ONION AND BUTTERNUT SQUASH

Serving Size: 6   Time: 1 hour 20 minutes

- 1 small butternut squash, peeled, seeded and chopped into ½-inch cubes
- 1 tablespoon coconut oil, melted
- 2 teaspoons each: sea salt and black pepper
- ½ large red onion, diced
- 2 medium zucchinis, diced
- 5 large eggs
- 5 egg yolks

1. Preheat the oven to 400 F.
2. Grease a medium-sized cast iron skillet with coconut oil. Toss in the cubed butternut squash with the melted coconut oil. Add the salt and pepper and cook until the squash is well coated.
3. Bake the squash for 25 minutes, or until fork tender.
4. Remove from the oven and add in the onion and zucchini. Stir to mix.
5. Whisk the eggs and egg yolks in a medium mixing bowl. Pour the eggs over the vegetables and season with more salt and pepper to taste.
6. Bake the frittata for 50–55 minutes, until the top is golden and set.
7. Allow to cool for 5–10 minutes before serving.

CINNAMON ROLLS WITH FROSTING

Serving Size: 8   Time: 25 minutes

Rolls:
- **1 cup almond flour**
- **2 tablespoons coconut flour**
- **½ teaspoon baking powder**
- **¼ teaspoon sea salt**
- **¼ cup coconut oil, melted**
- **¼ cup maple syrup**
- **3 eggs**
- **1 tablespoon vanilla extract**

Frosting:
- **2 tablespoons maple syrup**
- **1 tablespoon coconut oil, melted**
- **1 tablespoon cinnamon**
- **1 cup cream cheese**
- **⅔ cup unsalted grass-fed butter, softened**
- **1 teaspoon vanilla extract**
- **¼ cup coconut sugar**

1. Preheat the oven to 350 F.
2. Combine the almond and coconut flours, baking powder and salt together in a large bowl.
3. Combine the coconut oil, maple syrup, eggs and vanilla together in separate mixing bowl.
4. Combine both bowls and mix well.
5. Scoop the batter into a muffin pan with liners.
6. Mix together the first three frosting ingredients to make the cinnamon topping and sprinkle over the batter in the pan.
7. Bake 10–15 minutes, or until cooked through.
8. Mix the remaining cream cheese frosting ingredients together in a bowl.
9. Once the muffins have cooled, top with the cream cheese frosting.

TURKEY HASH

WITH EGGS, SWEET POTATO AND KALE

Serving Size: 4–6   Time: 20 minutes

- 4 tablespoons olive oil (divided)
- 2 medium sweet potatoes, peeled and grated
- 3 cups kale, chopped and stems removed
- ½ medium onion, finely diced
- 2 garlic cloves, smashed and minced
- 1 teaspoon of each: sea salt and black pepper
- 1 pound ground turkey
- 3 large eggs
- 3 egg yolks

1. Heat half of the olive oil in a medium skillet over medium-high heat. Add in the grated sweet potatoes, kale, onion, garlic, salt and pepper, stirring occasionally.
2. Brown the ground turkey in a medium skillet over medium heat, breaking up the meat and stirring continuously.
3. Add the turkey to the vegetables and stir to combine.
4. Whisk the eggs in a small bowl, pour into the skillet and stir continuously until the eggs are cooked through.
5. Add more salt and pepper to taste. Serve hot.

CHAPTER 2

Soups, Stews and Broths

DR. AXE BEEF BONE BROTH

Serving Size: 8   Time: 1–2 days

- **4 pounds beef bones**
- **4 carrots, chopped**
- **4 celery stalks, chopped**
- **2 medium onions, peel on, sliced in half lengthwise and quartered**
- **4 garlic cloves, peel on and smashed**
- **1 teaspoon sea salt**
- **1 teaspoon whole peppercorns**
- **½ cup olive oil**
- **2 bay leaves**
- **3 sprigs fresh thyme**
- **5–6 sprigs parsley**
- **18–20 cups cold water**

1. Place all ingredients in a 10-quart capacity crockpot.
2. Simmer for 24 to 48 hours, skimming fat occasionally.
3. Remove from the heat and allow to cool slightly. Discard the solids and strain the remainder in a bowl through a colander.
4. Let the broth cool to room temperature, cover and chill. Use within a week or freeze up to 3 months.

DR. AXE CHICKEN BONE BROTH

Serving Size: 10   Time: 1–2 days

- **4 pounds chicken necks/feet/wings**
- **3 carrots, chopped**
- **3 celery stalks, chopped**
- **2 medium onions, peel on, sliced in half lengthwise and quartered**
- **4 garlic cloves, peel on and smashed**
- **1 teaspoon Himalayan salt**
- **1 teaspoon whole peppercorns**
- **3 tablespoons apple cider vinegar**
- **2 bay leaves**
- **3 sprigs fresh thyme**
- **5–6 sprigs parsley**
- **1 teaspoon dried oregano**
- **18–20 cups cold water**

1. Place all ingredients in a 10-quart capacity crockpot. Set to low.
2. Simmer for 24 to 48 hours, skimming fat occasionally.
3. Remove from the heat and allow to cool slightly. Discard the solids and strain the remainder in a bowl through a colander.
4. Let the broth cool to room temperature, cover and chill. Use within a week or freeze up to 3 months.

POTATO LEEK SOUP

Serving Size: 10–12   **Time: 1 hour 10 minutes**

- 2 medium heads cauliflower
- ½ cup unsalted grass-fed butter
- 1 small red onion, diced
- 1 small yellow onion, diced
- 2 leeks, sliced
- 3 stalks of celery, chopped
- 2 medium Yukon potatoes, peeled and diced
- 1 bay leaf
- 3 sprigs fresh thyme
- 32 ounces chicken broth
- 2 cups vegetable broth
- 1 package uncured turkey bacon, diced
- Sliced 3–4 green onions
- Sea salt and black pepper to taste

1. Chop the cauliflower then add to a food processor and pulse until rice-like consistency. Set aside.
2. Melt the butter in a large saucepan over medium heat. Add in the onion, leeks and celery. Cover and cook for 10 minutes.
3. Stir in the potato, bay leaf and thyme. Cook for 10 minutes.
4. Add in the broths, cauliflower and turkey bacon, and bring the mixture to a boil.
5. Reduce heat and simmer for 30 minutes.
6. Remove from heat. Carefully remove the bay leaf and thyme.
7. Use an immersion hand blender to purée the soup in the pot (or purée in a high-speed blender). Allow the soup to rest for 5 minutes.
8. Top with the sliced green onions. Add the salt and pepper to taste.

Turmeric Detox Broth

TURMERIC DETOX BROTH

Serving Size: 10 **Time:** 1–2 days

- 4 pounds chicken thighs
- 3 carrots, chopped
- 2 medium onions, peel on, sliced in half lengthwise and quartered
- 4 garlic cloves, peel on and smashed
- 8–10 sprigs cilantro
- 1 teaspoon sea salt
- 1 teaspoon whole peppercorns
- 5 tablespoons ground turmeric
- 3 tablespoons olive oil
- 1 tablespoon apple cider vinegar
- One 3-inch piece fresh ginger, peeled and chopped
- 18–20 cups cold water

1. Place all ingredients in a 10-quart capacity crockpot.
2. Simmer for 24 to 48 hours, skimming the fat occasionally.
3. Remove from the heat and allow to cool slightly. Discard the solids and strain the remainder in a bowl through a colander.
4. Let the broth cool to room temperature, cover and chill. Use within a week or freeze up to 3 months.

CREAMY BUTTERNUT, TURMERIC AND GINGER SOUP

Serving Size: 4 **Time:** 40 minutes

- 2 tablespoons coconut oil
- 5 cups butternut squash, peeled and seeds removed
- 1 white onion, diced
- 2 tablespoons garlic, chopped
- 1 tablespoon ginger, grated
- 1 teaspoon each: ground turmeric, sea salt and black pepper
- 1 cup bone broth
- 1 cup full-fat coconut milk

1. Heat the coconut oil in a large soup pot over medium-high heat.
2. Once the oil is hot, add the squash, onion, garlic and ginger and sauté for 3–4 minutes.
3. Add the turmeric, salt, pepper and bone broth and let simmer for 15–20 minutes, or until the squash is softened.
4. Carefully add the soup mixture to a high-speed blender and blend until smooth.
5. Add the mixture back to the soup pot and stir in the coconut milk. Let simmer for 10–15 more minutes and serve while hot.

CURRIED CAULIFLOWER SOUP

Serving Size: 6–8   **Time: 40 minutes**

- 1 tablespoon unsalted grass-fed butter or coconut oil
- 1 head cauliflower, cut into medium pieces
- 1 leek, chopped (white and green parts separated)
- 2 medium kohlrabi, peeled and diced
- 4 cups low-sodium chicken broth
- ½ teaspoon sea salt
- One 2-inch knob turmeric, peeled, washed and grated
- One 2-inch knob ginger, peeled, washed and grated
- 2 tablespoons curry powder: yellow, Maharajah or Ras el Hanout
- 1–2 teaspoons cayenne pepper (optional)
- Zest of 1 lemon
- Juice of 1 lemon
- 5 cloves garlic, minced or pressed
- 1 rotisserie chicken, skinned and deboned
- Two 13.5-ounce cans full-fat coconut milk
- 1 tablespoon coconut sugar (optional)

1. Heat the butter or oil in a large pot or dutch oven over medium heat until the butter is melted or the oil is shimmering.
2. Add the cauliflower, white parts of the leek and kohlrabi. Sauté for 5–8 minutes, stirring often.
3. Increase the heat to medium-high. Add the chicken broth, salt, turmeric, ginger, curry powder and optional cayenne pepper. Cover and bring the soup to a low boil.
4. Once the soup is boiling, set aside the lemon zest and stir in the lemon juice, green parts of the leek, garlic, chicken, coconut milk and optional coconut sugar. Decrease the heat to low and simmer for 10 minutes.
5. Taste the soup and add more salt if needed. Simmer another 10 minutes. Remove the pot from the heat and stir in the lemon zest. Allow the soup to rest for 5 minutes before serving. Soup flavor will continue to improve over the next few days.

EGG DROP SOUP

Serving Size: 4   Time: 15 minutes

- **8 cups chicken bone broth**
- **2 baby bok choy, thinly sliced**
- **½ cup sliced mushrooms**
- **1 tablespoon ground ginger**
- **1 tablespoon Bragg's liquid aminos**
- **1 teaspoon sea salt**
- **1 teaspoon ground white pepper**
- **4 large eggs**
- **2 egg yolks**
- **1 bunch green onions, thinly sliced**

1. Pour the broth into a medium pot and bring to a very low simmer. Add in the bok choy, mushrooms, ginger, liquid aminos, salt and pepper and simmer for 10–12 minutes.
2. Whisk the eggs and egg yolks in a small bowl and, holding a fork over the bowl, gently pour the eggs through the tines of the fork.
3. Lightly whisk the broth and gently stir in the green onions.
4. Ladle into bowls and top with more green onions if desired.

CREAMY BROCCOLI SOUP

Serving Size: 2   Time: 30 minutes

- **2 tablespoons coconut oil**
- **2 medium green onions, coarsely chopped**
- **2 cloves garlic, minced**
- **1 large head fresh broccoli, chopped**
- **1 tablespoon dried basil**
- **2 cups chopped spinach, kale, turnip greens, collards or Swiss chard**
- **1½ cups full-fat coconut milk**
- **2 cups chicken bone broth**
- **1 teaspoon sea salt**
- **1 tablespoon curry powder**

1. Melt the coconut oil in large soup pan over medium heat and sauté the green onions and garlic for 1–2 minutes, until translucent.
2. Stir in the chopped broccoli. Sauté until the broccoli turns bright green, stirring frequently.
3. Add the basil and additional chopped greens. Cover and steam-sauté for 3–4 more minutes.
4. Transfer the vegetables to a food processor or high-speed blender. If using a blender, process in two batches. Add a little coconut milk and process until smooth.
5. Transfer the puréed vegetables back to the pot and add the remaining coconut milk along with the broth, salt and curry powder. Reheat gently over medium heat and stir. Serve.

Chicken Teriyaki Soup

CHICKEN TERIYAKI SOUP

Serving Size: 4   Time: 20–25 minutes

- 8 cups chicken bone broth
- 1 teaspoon ground ginger
- 2–4 tablespoons Bragg's liquid aminos
- 2 baby bok choy, thinly sliced
- ½ medium red onion, sliced
- 2 large carrots, spiralized into noodles
- 3 cups cooked, shredded chicken
- 1 teaspoon each: sea salt and black pepper
- 2–3 green onions, thinly sliced

1. Heat the broth in a medium pot until just simmering.
2. Add in the ginger and aminos and simmer for 1–2 minutes, stirring continuously.
3. Add in the bok choy, onion, carrots, chicken, salt and pepper.
4. Simmer for 15–20 minutes. Ladle into bowls and top with the green onions.

MISO MUSHROOM SOUP

Serving Size: 2   Time: 25 minutes

- 4 cups bone broth or water
- 2 tablespoons mellow white miso
- 2 cups fresh mushrooms or ½ cup dried, chopped
- 1 large yellow or red onion, diced
- 2 cloves garlic, pressed or minced
- 1–2 teaspoons ginger, grated
- 2 cups chopped collard greens
- 2 tablespoons coconut aminos

1. Heat the bone broth or water in a medium pot over medium-high heat. Once simmering, remove about half a cup and whisk together with the miso, incorporating until smooth.
2. Add the miso mixture back to the pot along with the mushrooms, onion, garlic, ginger, collards and coconut aminos. Return to a simmer and decrease the heat to low, simmering gently for 20 minutes.

BUTTERNUT SQUASH SOUP

Serving Size: 4   Time: 45 minutes

- **4 tablespoons unsalted grass-fed butter**
- **1 onion, chopped**
- **1 Granny Smith apple, peeled, cored and chopped**
- **2 teaspoons dried sage**
- **1 butternut squash, peeled, seeded and cut into chunks**
- **4 cups chicken bone broth**
- **¼–½ cup full-fat coconut milk**
- **Dash of nutmeg**
- **Sea salt and black pepper to taste**

1. Melt the butter in a pot over medium heat. Add the onion, apple and sage. Cook, stirring occasionally, for 8 minutes.
2. Add the squash and broth. Bring to a simmer and cook until the squash is tender, 15–20 minutes.
3. Transfer mixture to a high-speed blender (or use an immersion blender), working in batches if necessary, and purée until smooth. (Be careful blending hot liquids.)
4. Return to the pot and stir in coconut milk to reach desired consistency. Heat through and season with the nutmeg, salt and pepper to taste before serving.

GROUND TURKEY, SWEET POTATO AND ONION SOUP

Serving Size: 4   Time: 40 minutes

- **1 pound ground turkey**
- **1.5 pounds sweet potato, diced**
- **1 cup diced red onion**
- **½ cup parsley, chopped**
- **1 teaspoon of each: sea salt and black pepper**
- **½ teaspoon ground turmeric**
- **4 cups bone broth**
- **1 tablespoon lime zest**

1. Add the ground turkey to a stockpot and use a spatula to chop it up. Add the sweet potato and onion and cook for another 5 minutes.
2. Add the parsley, salt, pepper and turmeric and mix thoroughly.
3. Add the bone broth and cook for 20–25 minutes, or until the sweet potatoes are softened.
4. Stir in the lime zest and serve while hot.

Butternut Squash Soup

Carrot Fennel Soup

CARROT FENNEL SOUP

Serving Size: 4   Time: 50 minutes

- 1 tablespoon coconut oil
- 2 pounds carrots
- 1 fennel bulb, coarsely chopped
- 1 yellow onion, coarsely chopped
- 2 large garlic cloves, chopped
- 1 teaspoon each: sea salt and black pepper
- 2 cups bone broth (divided)

1. Heat the coconut oil in a large soup pot and add the carrots, fennel, onion, garlic, salt and pepper. Sauté for 6–8 minutes.
2. Add 1 cup of bone broth to the soup pot and put a lid on it. Let the carrot mixture simmer for 25–30 minutes, or until the carrots are softened.
3. Carefully add the soup mixture to a high-speed blender and blend until smooth.
4. Add it back to the pot and whisk in the remaining cup of bone broth. Let cook for another 5 minutes and then serve.

ROASTED PUMPKIN GINGER APPLE SOUP

Serving Size: 4–6   Time: 25–40 minutes

- 3 tablespoons olive oil (divided)
- 1 medium sugar pumpkin, cut in half lengthwise and seeds removed
- 1 medium yellow onion, chopped
- 2 large apples, peeled, cored and diced
- 1 teaspoon ginger, freshly grated
- 3 cloves garlic, smashed
- 4 cups chicken bone broth
- 1 teaspoon each: sea salt and black pepper

1. Preheat the oven to 400 F. Drizzle half of the olive oil on a baking sheet lined with parchment paper and place the pumpkin face down.
2. Bake for 30 minutes or until flesh is soft. Remove from the oven and allow to cool. Remove skin.
3. While the pumpkin is roasting, line another baking sheet with parchment paper and add the onion, apples, ginger and garlic. Drizzle with the remaining olive oil and place in the oven, baking for 20 minutes.
4. Place all roasted ingredients in a high-speed blender. Add in the broth, salt and pepper. Purée until smooth and creamy. Serve immediately.

CREAMY CARROT, TURMERIC, GARLIC AND ONION SOUP

Serving Size: 4   Time: 45 minutes

- 1 tablespoon coconut oil
- 2 pounds carrots, chopped
- 2 small onions, chopped
- 4 garlic cloves, chopped
- 1 cup bone broth
- 1 teaspoon each: turmeric, sea salt and black pepper
- 1 cup full-fat coconut milk
- Pumpkin seeds to taste

1. Heat the coconut oil in a large soup pot over medium-high heat. Add the carrots, onions and garlic and sauté for 2–3 minutes.
2. Add the bone broth, and then put the lid on the pot and cook for 20–25 minutes, or until the carrots are softened.
3. Add the turmeric, salt and pepper and mix together.
4. Add the carrot and bone broth mixture to a high-speed blender and blend until smooth.
5. Add the soup mixture back to pot and whisk in the coconut milk and simmer for another 8–10 minutes. Garnish with the pumpkin seeds and serve.

French Onion Soup

FRENCH ONION SOUP

Serving Size: 4–6   **Time: 8–10 hours**

- 6 tablespoons unsalted grass-fed butter
- 4 onions, thinly sliced
- 1 tablespoon raw honey
- 3 garlic cloves, pressed or minced
- ¼ cup apple cider vinegar
- 7 cups beef broth
- 1 tablespoon sea salt
- ¼ teaspoon fresh thyme
- 2 bay leaves
- ½ cup goat cheese, shredded (optional)

1. Heat the butter in a large pot over medium-high heat. Stir in the onions until translucent. Add the honey and reduce the heat to medium, allowing to cook for 30 minutes.
2. Add the garlic and apple cider vinegar. Transfer the mixture to a crockpot and add in the remaining ingredients, except the goat cheese.
3. Cook on low for 8–10 hours. Garnish with the cheese to serve.

LEAN BEEF AND SAUERKRAUT SOUP

Serving Size: 10–12   **Time: 1 hour 30 minutes**

- 1 tablespoon coconut oil
- 1 pound lean beef
- 1 medium white onion, small diced
- 2 carrots, chopped
- 2 stalks celery, chopped
- 2 cloves garlic, smashed and chopped
- ⅛ cup apple cider vinegar
- 10 cups beef bone broth
- 4½ cups sauerkraut
- 1 teaspoon each: sea salt and black pepper

1. Heat the coconut oil in a large stock pot over medium heat. Add in the beef, onion, carrots, celery and garlic, stirring occasionally until the beef begins to brown, about 8 minutes.
2. Add in the apple cider vinegar and continue stirring another couple of minutes.
3. Add in the broth, sauerkraut, salt and pepper. Bring to a boil and then let simmer for 1 hour.
4. Allow the soup to rest for 10 minutes before serving. Add more salt and pepper to taste.

TURKEY MEATBALL SOUP

Serving Size: 2–4   Time: 1 hour

Meatballs:
- **1 pound ground turkey**
- **2 eggs**
- **¼ cup minced onion**
- **1 teaspoon minced garlic**
- **½ teaspoon onion powder**
- **Sea salt and black pepper to taste**
- **⅓ cup coconut flour**

Soup:
- **2–3 tablespoons ghee**
- **½ cup chopped onions**
- **1–2 cups each: chopped celery and chopped carrots**
- **4 cups chicken bone broth**
- **1 teaspoon thyme**
- **¾ teaspoon each: sage and rosemary**
- **Sea salt to taste**

1. Mix the meatball ingredients together in a bowl. Form into small meatballs.
2. Add the ghee, onions, celery and carrots in a stock pot over medium-high heat and cook until the onions are translucent.
3. Pour the bone broth into the stock pot and bring the mixture to a simmer. Add the remaining seasonings.
4. Carefully drop the meatballs into the simmering broth and cook for an additional 45 minutes.

ACORN SQUASH BISQUE

Serving Size: 6–8   Time: 1 hour 5 minutes

- **1 tablespoon coconut oil**
- **2 acorn squash**
- **1 butternut squash**
- **Sea salt and black pepper to taste**
- **3 carrots, chopped**
- **½ white onion, sliced**
- **1 clove garlic, peeled and chopped**
- **1 green apple, peeled, cored and sliced**
- **1 tablespoon unsalted grass-fed butter**
- **½ tablespoon each: ground ginger, ground cinnamon and nutmeg**
- **5 cups vegetable broth**

1. Heat the oven to 425 F. Grease two baking sheets with the coconut oil. Slice the acorn and butternut squashes lengthwise (through the stem) and remove the seeds.

2. Season the squash meat with the salt and pepper. Place the squash halves facedown on the baking sheets.

3. Arrange the carrots, onion, garlic and apple around the squash halves on the baking sheets. Bake for 40 minutes.

4. Allow the squash to cool slightly before handling. Scoop the flesh from the squash halves and add to a high-speed blender, along with the carrots, onion, garlic, apple, butter, ginger, cinnamon and nutmeg. Blend well.

5. Bring the vegetable broth to a boil in a medium saucepan over medium-high heat.

6. Reduce the heat to medium and stir in the blended squash mixture until well incorporated.

7. Cook the bisque for 5 minutes, then reduce the heat and simmer for 10 minutes.

8. Remove from the heat. Add more salt and pepper to taste. Best served warm/hot.

CHICKEN "ZOODLE" SOUP

Serving Size: 6–8   Time: 55 minutes

- 3 chicken breasts
- 2 tablespoons olive oil (divided)
- 1 teaspoon each: sea salt and black pepper
- ½ medium red onion, diced
- 3 stalks celery, chopped
- 6 carrots, chopped
- 4 cups chopped kale, stems removed
- 8 cups chicken bone broth
- 3 medium zucchini, spiralized into noodles
- Fresh basil or parsley

1. Preheat oven to 325 F. Line a baking sheet with parchment paper. Place the chicken on the sheet, drizzle with half of the olive oil and add the salt and pepper. Place in the oven and let bake for 25–30 minutes.
2. Add the remainder of the olive oil, onion, celery and carrots in a large stock pot and cook over medium heat for 8–10 minutes. Add in the kale and broth. Turn the heat to low and let simmer for 25 minutes.
3. Take the chicken out of the oven and allow to cool for 5 minutes. Using two forks, shred the chicken and add to the stock pot. Simmer for another 15 minutes.
4. Using a spiralizer, zoodle your zucchini into noodles (each zucchini is enough for two servings). Place a serving of noodles in a soup bowl and scoop out the soup to pour over the "zoodles."
5. Add more salt and pepper to taste. Top with the basil or parsley. Serve hot.

75

Kale and Butternut Chicken Soup

KALE AND BUTTERNUT CHICKEN SOUP

Serving Size: 4 **Time: 45 minutes**

- 1 tablespoon coconut oil
- 4 cups chopped and peeled butternut squash
- 4 cups chopped kale, stems removed
- 1 cup diced red onion
- 3 cups shredded chicken
- 4 cups chicken bone broth
- 2 tablespoons chopped garlic
- 1 teaspoon each: sea salt and black pepper
- ½ teaspoon ground turmeric

1. Heat the coconut oil in a large soup pot over medium-high heat. Add the squash, kale and onion and sauté for 3–4 minutes.
2. Add the chicken, broth, garlic, salt, pepper and turmeric and stir.
3. Put a lid on the soup pot and let simmer over medium heat for 25–30 minutes, or until the squash is cooked through.

SLOW COOKER BISON, CARROT AND CABBAGE STEW

Serving Size: 4 **Time: 4 hours 30 minutes**

- 2½–3 pounds bison shoulder roast
- 1 tablespoon coconut oil
- 2 teaspoons sea salt (divided)
- 1 teaspoon black pepper
- 2 celeriac roots, peeled and coarsely chopped
- 8 carrots, coarsely chopped
- 1 yellow onion, coarsely chopped
- 4 large garlic cloves, chopped
- 1 cup beef bone broth
- 4 cups chopped green cabbage

1. Heat the coconut oil in a large skillet over medium-high heat.
2. Sprinkle the bison roast with 1 teaspoon of the salt and the pepper. Place in the hot skillet. Sear both sides for 2 minutes and then place in the slow cooker.
3. Add the celeriac roots, carrots, onion, garlic, remaining salt and broth. Set the crockpot to high.
4. Cook the roast for 3 hours, and then add the chopped cabbage and cook for 1 more hour.
5. Serve the roast as is or over a bed of Cauliflower Rice (page 92).

BEEF "BAGA" STEW

Serving Size: 3–6   Time: 8–10 hours

- 1–2 pounds beef chuck
- Sea salt and black pepper to taste
- 2 onions, peeled and chopped
- 6 cloves garlic
- 6 sprigs fresh parsley, chopped
- 6 sprigs fresh thyme, chopped
- 6 cups beef bone broth
- 4 carrots, chopped
- 2 rutabagas, peeled and chopped
- 4 stalks celery, chopped
- 2–4 tablespoons coconut aminos

1. Add all ingredients to a crockpot and cook on low for 8–10 hours.

CHICKEN GINGER LEMONGRASS SOUP

Serving Size: 4   Time: 6 hours 30 minutes

- 1 pound boneless, skinless chicken breasts
- 3 cups chicken bone broth
- 2 cups cabbage, chopped
- 1 cup mushrooms, sliced
- 4 carrots, chopped
- ⅓ cup onion, sliced
- ¼ cup fresh lemon juice
- 2 stalks lemongrass, smashed, or zest of 1 lemon, cut into strips
- 4 cloves garlic, minced
- 1 knob fresh ginger, peeled and minced
- Sea salt to taste

1. Combine all ingredients in a slow cooker. Cook on low for 6–8 hours.
2. Remove and discard the lemongrass or lemon zest. Shred the chicken in the mixture and stir to distribute. Season with the salt to taste.

CHAPTER 3

Side Dishes and Dressings

SPAGHETTI SQUASH AND SAUERKRAUT

Serving Size: 4–6   Time: 55 minutes

- **2 tablespoons olive oil (divided)**
- **1 large spaghetti squash**
- **1 teaspoon each: sea salt and black pepper**
- **1 cup sauerkraut**

1. Preheat the oven to 375 F. Line a baking sheet with parchment paper and drizzle with half of the olive oil. Cut the spaghetti squash in half, lengthwise, and place face down on the baking sheet.
2. Cook for 30–40 minutes, or until the squash is easily pierced with a fork.
3. Let cool for 5 minutes. Scrape out the spaghetti strands into a bowl.
4. Add in the salt, pepper and sauerkraut. Mix well. Drizzle the remaining olive oil and serve immediately.

MAPLE GLAZED ROSEMARY CARROTS

Serving Size: 4–6   Time: 25 minutes

- **3 cups carrots, peeled and sliced**
- **2 tablespoons coconut oil**
- **2 tablespoons maple syrup**
- **1½ tablespoons chopped fresh rosemary**
- **½ teaspoon each: sea salt and black pepper**

1. Cook the carrots in a skillet with just enough water to cover them. Bring to a boil over medium heat and simmer until the water has evaporated and the carrots are soft.
2. Stir in the coconut oil, maple syrup, rosemary, salt and pepper and cook for another 5–10 minutes over low heat.

Maple Glazed Rosemary Carrots

SWEET POTATO FRIES

Serving Size: 3–6   Time: 1 hour

- 1–1½ pounds sweet potatoes
- ¼ cup coconut oil, melted
- ½ teaspoon sea salt
- ½ teaspoon paprika
- ¼ teaspoon cinnamon

1. Preheat the oven to 425 F. Peel the potatoes and cut into strips about ½-inch wide on each side.
2. Place all ingredients in a sealable plastic bag and shake until the potatoes are completely coated. Spread onto a baking sheet.
3. Cook for 30–45 minutes, turning every 10 minutes.
4. Transfer immediately to a paper towel-lined plate and serve warm.

SWEET POTATO AND CAULIFLOWER MASH

Serving Size: 6–8   Time: 25 minutes

- 6 sweet potatoes, peeled and cubed
- 1 medium head cauliflower, cored and chopped
- ⅓ cup vegetable broth
- 4 tablespoons ghee
- 1 teaspoon each: sea salt and black pepper

1. Bring a large pot of water to a boil. Add in the sweet potatoes and cauliflower and cook for 15–20 minutes, or until fork tender.
2. Once the vegetables are finished boiling, strain most of the water and add in the broth, ghee, salt and pepper.
3. Use a standing mixer or potato masher to mix/mash all ingredients until well combined. Add more salt and pepper to taste.

GRILLED ASPARAGUS

Serving Size: 2–3   Time: 15 minutes

- 3 tablespoons coconut oil
- 1 bunch asparagus
- 5 cloves garlic, chopped

1. Melt the coconut oil in a skillet over medium-high heat.
2. Add the asparagus and garlic to the pan. Cover and cook for 10 minutes, stirring occasionally. Continue to cook until desired tenderness is achieved.

MASHED CAUL-TATOES

Serving Size: 4   Time: 25 minutes

- 1 medium head cauliflower
- 4 tablespoons ghee
- ½ teaspoon each: sea salt and black pepper
- Pinch of parsley

1. Steam the cauliflower for 10 minutes or until the florets are tender.
2. Add the cauliflower to a food processor along with the ghee, salt and pepper and purée until smooth.
3. Serve immediately, topping with the parsley.

Grilled Asparagus

Mashed Caul-Tatoes

BAKED CAULIFLOWER

Serving Size: 4   Time: 45 minutes

- 1 large head of cauliflower, chopped into large sections
- ¼ cup almond flour
- ¼ cup coconut oil, melted
- ½ teaspoon garlic powder
- ⅛ teaspoon sea salt
- 1 pinch each: red pepper flakes and dried oregano

1. Place the head of cauliflower in a pot with an inch of water. Cover and boil over medium heat for 20 minutes, or until tender. (Watch to see that the water doesn't completely evaporate.)
2. Preheat the oven to 375 F. Mix the flour and coconut oil in a bowl.
3. Place the cauliflower in a baking dish and coat with the seasonings.
4. Bake for 10–15 minutes, or until golden brown.

Ghee-Baked Brussels Sprouts

GHEE-BAKED BRUSSELS SPROUTS

Serving Size: 1–2   Time: 45 minutes

- 1 bunch Brussels sprouts, halved
- 1 small red onion, cut into crescents
- ½ cup walnuts, chopped
- 2 tablespoons ghee or coconut oil, melted
- Sea salt and black pepper to taste

1. Preheat the oven to 425 F.
2. Combine the Brussels sprouts, onion and walnuts in a bowl and mix in the ghee until evenly distributed.
3. Sprinkle with the salt and pepper and spread the mixture out on a rimmed baking sheet.
4. Roast until slightly browned, about 25–40 minutes.

ZUCCHINI FRIES

Serving Size: 2   Time: 40 minutes

- 1 teaspoon coconut oil, melted
- 3 egg whites
- ¼ cup full-fat coconut milk
- 1 cup each: almond flour and coconut flour
- 1 tablespoon each: Himalayan salt and black pepper
- 3 zucchinis, cut in half and quartered

1. Preheat the oven to 375 F. Line a baking sheet with parchment paper, grease with the coconut oil and set aside.
2. Whisk the egg whites and milk in a bowl.
3. Mix the flours, salt and pepper in a separate bowl.
4. Dunk the quartered zucchinis in the egg white/milk mixture then dunk in the flour/seasoning mixture.
5. Place the zucchinis on the baking sheet. Bake for 30–35 minutes, or until the fries are golden brown. Add more salt and pepper to taste. Serve hot.

CAULIFLOWER RICE

Serving Size: 4   **Time: 15 minutes**

- 1 head of cauliflower, chopped
- 2 teaspoons coconut oil
- ½ teaspoon each: sea salt and black pepper
- ¼ cup bone broth or stock
- Fresh parsley

1. Process the cauliflower in a food processor until rice-like.
2. Heat a large saucepan to medium-high heat and add the coconut oil.
3. Once the coconut oil is hot ,add the riced cauliflower and sauté for 5 minutes.
4. Add the bone broth to the rice. Stir and then place the lid on and let cook for another 3-4 minutes.
5. Take the lid off and cook for another 2 minutes, and then serve with the fresh parsley.

Baked Vegetable Fries

BAKED VEGETABLE FRIES

Serving Size: 2–4   Time: 45 minutes

- **1 rutabaga**
- **3–4 carrots**
- **1 red bell pepper**
- **1 onion**
- **1 cup chopped portabello mushrooms**
- **2 tablespoons ghee or coconut oil**
- **1–2 teaspoons sea salt**
- **2 teaspoons each: black pepper, onion powder and garlic powder**

1. Preheat the oven to 425 F.
2. Cut the vegetables into thin long strips.
3. Coat in the ghee or coconut oil. Sprinkle with the salt, pepper, onion powder and garlic powder.
4. Bake in the oven for 40 minutes.

ROASTED YELLOW SQUASH AND ONIONS

Serving Size: 4–6   Time: 30 minutes

- **6 medium yellow squash, peeled and sliced**
- **1 medium white onion, sliced**
- **2 tablespoons olive oil**
- **1 teaspoon each: sea salt and black pepper**

1. Preheat the oven to 350 F. Add all ingredients in a casserole dish, using your hands to mix evenly.
2. Bake for 20–25 minutes, or until the squash is tender.
3. Remove from the oven and let cool for 5 minutes before serving. Add more salt and pepper to taste.

AVOCADO RANCH DRESSING

Serving Size: 4   **Time: 35 minutes**

- **1 cup goat milk kefir**
- **2 tablespoons chopped scallions (green tops)**
- **2 teaspoons each: chopped fresh thyme and chopped fresh parsley**
- **1 teaspoon fresh dill, chopped**
- **2 teaspoons roasted garlic**
- **¼ teaspoon each: onion powder and paprika**
- **⅛ teaspoon cayenne pepper**
- **Cracked black pepper and sea salt to taste**
- **2 very ripe avocados**

1. Combine all of the ingredients, except the avocados, in a small bowl and blend well with a wire whisk. Cover with plastic wrap and allow to sit at room temperature for 30 minutes to 1 hour to let the flavors marry.
2. Add in kefir mixture and avocados in a high-speed blender and purée on high.
3. Refrigerate any remaining dressing. Dressing will keep for 3–5 days without the avocados and 1–2 days with the avocados.

SAUTÉED SPINACH

WITH GARLIC

Serving Size: 4   Time: 10 minutes

- 1 tablespoon coconut oil
- 3 cloves garlic, minced
- 8–10 cups spinach
- Sea salt and black pepper to taste

1. Melt the coconut oil in a large pot over medium heat. Add in the garlic and stir for 2 minutes. Add in the spinach, salt and pepper, stirring until the spinach becomes wilted, about 5 minutes.
2. Add more salt and pepper to taste. Serve hot.

BUTTERNUT SQUASH, TURKEY BACON AND ONION

Serving Size: 4–6   Time: 35 minutes

- 2 medium butternut squash, peeled, seeded and chopped into 1-inch cubes
- 1 medium white onion, sliced
- 2 cloves garlic, smashed and minced
- 1 package uncured turkey bacon, chopped
- 2 tablespoons olive oil
- 1 teaspoon each: sea salt and black pepper

1. Preheat the oven to 350 F. Add all ingredients in a casserole dish, using your hands to mix evenly.
2. Bake for 30 minutes, or until the squash is tender.
3. Remove from the oven and let cool for 5 minutes before serving. Add the salt and pepper to taste.

Sautéed Spinach

Coconut Oil Mayonnaise

COCONUT OIL MAYONNAISE

Serving Size: 12–16   **Time: 10 minutes**

- **3 egg yolks at room temperature**
- **1 teaspoon German or Dijon mustard**
- **1½ teaspoons fresh lemon juice**
- **2 tablespoons apple cider vinegar**
- **Pinch of sea salt and black pepper**
- **¾ cup coconut oil, melted**

1. Blend all ingredients, except the coconut oil, in a blender at a very low speed.
2. Slowly drizzle in the oil and mix for at least a minute.
3. Scoop into a container and screw the lid on very tightly. Leave the mayo out on counter for 7 hours before refrigerating.

HONEY MUSTARD DRESSING

Serving Size: 4   **Time: 5 minutes**

- **¼ cup German or Dijon mustard, preferably with an apple cider vinegar base (as opposed to distilled white vinegar)**
- **3 tablespoons raw honey**
- **2 tablespoons goat milk yogurt or puréed soaked cashews**
- **½ teaspoon horseradish**
- **Dash of sea salt**
- **1 tablespoon chopped fresh tarragon (optional)**

1. Whisk all of the ingredients together in a small bowl until smooth.
2. Store the dressing in a sealed bottle or jar in the refrigerator for up to 7 days.

CASHEW CAESAR DRESSING

Serving Size: 2–3   Time: 5 minutes

- **1 cup raw cashews, soaked at least 3 hours or overnight and rinsed very well**
- **2 teaspoons mellow white miso paste**
- **2 teaspoons Dijon mustard**
- **1 teaspoon Worcestershire sauce**
- **1 clove garlic**
- **Zest of 1 lemon**
- **1–2 tablespoons lemon juice**
- **Sea salt and cracked black pepper to taste**
- **Water**

1. Place all ingredients in a high-speed blender and blend well, adding only enough water to facilitate blending.
2. Store unused dressing in a sealed container in the refrigerator for up to 5 days.

BAKED PEAR AND ARUGULA SALAD

Serving Size: 4   Time: 50 minutes

- **Juice of two lemons**
- **1 tablespoon apple cider vinegar**
- **¼ cup olive oil (divided)**
- **⅓ cup raw honey**
- **4 ripe pears, cored and quartered**
- **1 teaspoon coconut oil**
- **6 cups arugula**
- **1 cup Medjool dates, pitted and chopped**
- **1 cup fresh blueberries**
- **Himalayan pink salt and black pepper to taste**

1. Preheat the oven to 375 F. Combine the lemon juice, apple cider vinegar, half of the olive oil and honey in a medium bowl. Mix well.
2. Allow the pears to soak in the mixture for 15 minutes.
3. Arrange the marinated pears in an 8 x 8 baking dish. Bake the marinated pears, basting every 10 minutes with the remaining mixture, for 40–50 minutes, or until fork tender.
4. For the dressing, whisk the remaining olive oil and basting mixture and set aside.
5. Quickly sauté (in a little bit of coconut oil) or steam the arugula for 2–4 minutes.
6. Arrange the arugula, dates and blueberries onto four plates. Top each plate with three roasted pears and drizzle with the dressing. Add the Himalayan salt and pepper to taste. Serve immediately.

ORANGE TAHINI

Serving Size: 4   Time: 5 minutes

- **Zest of 1 large orange**
- **Juice of 1 large orange**
- **3 tablespoons coconut oil, melted**
- **3 tablespoons tahini**
- **1 teaspoon garlic powder or granules**
- **½ teaspoon coriander**
- **⅛ teaspoon cinnamon**
- **1 tablespoon fresh cilantro, chopped**

1. Whisk together all ingredients, except the cilantro, in a small bowl. Continue whisking until smooth. Stir in the cilantro.
2. Store the dressing in a sealed bottle or jar in the refrigerator for up to 5 days. Before use, allow the dressing to come to room temperature so the coconut oil liquefies.

BRAISED CABBAGE

Serving Size: 4–6   Time: 45 minutes

- **2 teaspoons olive oil**
- **2 medium white onions, cut and thinly sliced**
- **1 carrot, cut into thin rounds**
- **1 clove garlic, minced**
- **1 Savoy cabbage, halved, cored and thinly sliced**
- **1 cup chicken bone broth**
- **¼ cup apple cider vinegar**
- **Sea salt and black pepper to taste**

1. Heat the oil in a large pot over medium heat. Add in the onions, carrot and garlic. Cook, stirring until the onions start to turn golden, about 8 minutes.
2. Add in the cabbage and cook, stirring occasionally, until the cabbage wilts, about 5 minutes.
3. Add in the broth and bring to a simmer. Cover and cook over low heat until tender, 20–25 minutes.
4. Uncover and add in the apple cider vinegar. Increase the heat to high, and cook for 8 to 10 minutes. Season with the salt and pepper to taste. Serve hot.

CHAPTER 4

Main Dishes

SALMON CAKES

Serving Size: 1–2   Time: 15 minutes

- 1 can Alaskan salmon (wild-caught)
- 2 eggs
- 1 tablespoon olive oil
- ¼ white onion, chopped
- ¼ cup almond flour*
- 1 teaspoon each: sea salt and black pepper

1. Place all ingredients in a bowl and mix together. Form into patties.
2. Cook 5–8 minutes on each side, or until browned. Plate and serve.

*Add more almond flour if needed to form cakes.

ROASTED SALMON
WITH KEFIR, GARLIC AND AVOCADO SAUCE

Serving Size: 4   Time: 45 minutes

Fish:
- 1½ pounds salmon fillet, wild-caught, skin on, pin bones removed
- 2 tablespoons olive oil
- ½ teaspoon sea salt
- ½–1 teaspoon black pepper
- 2 tablespoons lemon juice

Sauce:
- 1 avocado, peeled and pitted
- 2 cups kefir
- 2 cloves garlic, peeled and smashed
- ¼–½ teaspoon sea salt

1. Preheat the oven to 425 F. Place the salmon on a baking sheet lined with parchment paper, rub with the olive oil and coat evenly with the salt and pepper. Drizzle on the lemon juice. Cook for 15 minutes, or until it flakes when gently pressed.
2. While the salmon is roasting, add the avocado, kefir, garlic and salt to a high-speed blender and blend on high until well combined. Add more kefir if necessary.
3. Remove the salmon from the oven. Peel skin off and break flesh into chunks. Plate and drizzle with sauce. Serve immediately.

ZUCCHINI NOODLE NOURISH BOWL

WITH CHICKEN AND VEGETABLES

Serving Size: 2   Time: 10 minutes

Dressing:
- **5–6 tablespoons Cauliflower Hummus (page 153)**
- **1 tablespoon apple cider vinegar**
- **1 teaspoon lemon juice**

Bowl:
- **½ head cauliflower**
- **1 tablespoon olive oil**
- **½ medium red onion, thinly sliced**
- **2 carrots, shredded**
- **1½ cups chopped chicken**
- **2–3 cups chopped kale, stems removed**
- **½ teaspoon each: Himalayan salt and black pepper**
- **1 zucchini, spiralized into noodles**
- **1 cup kimchi or sauerkraut**
- **1 avocado, peeled, pitted and sliced (divided)**

1. Mix the Cauliflower Hummus, apple cider vinegar and lemon juice in a small bowl. Cover and refrigerate.
2. Process the cauliflower in a food processor until rice-like.
3. Heat the olive oil in a pan over medium heat. Add the cauliflower rice, onion, carrots, chicken, kale, salt and pepper, continuously stirring for about 5-6 minutes, or until the kale wilts and the chicken is cooked through.
4. Using a spiralizer, zoodle your zucchini into noodles (each zucchini is enough for two servings). Place a serving of noodles into a bowl and evenly distribute the cooked vegetables from pan.
5. Add more salt and pepper to taste. Top with the kimchi or sauerkraut, sliced avocado and dressing. Serve.

CAULIFLOWER RICE STIR-FRY

WITH CHICKEN, AVOCADO AND LIME

Serving Size: 4	Time: 30 minutes

- **1 tablespoon coconut oil**
- **2–3 carrots, thinly sliced**
- **1 zucchini, sliced**
- **1 red onion, diced**
- **1 head cauliflower, riced**
- **3–4 chicken breasts, cooked and shredded**
- **2 large garlic cloves, chopped**
- **1 teaspoon sea salt**
- **½ teaspoon black pepper**
- **¼ cup cilantro, chopped**
- **Zest of 1 lime**
- **J uice of 1 lime**
- **1 avocado, sliced**

1. Heat a large skillet to medium-high heat and add the coconut oil.
2. Add the sliced carrots, zucchini and red onion and cook for 6–8 minutes.
3. Add the cauliflower rice and cook for another minute. Then add the shredded chicken, garlic, salt, pepper, cilantro, lime zest and juice.
4. Mix thoroughly and let the mixture cook for another 5–8 minutes. Serve with the avocado slices on top.

ROASTED CHICKEN
WITH GHEE AND GARLIC

Serving Size: 4   Time: 40 minutes

- **2 teaspoons coconut oil**
- **2 pounds chicken thighs, skin on and bone in**
- **2 tablespoons ghee**
- **2 tablespoons minced garlic**
- **½ teaspoon each: sea salt and black pepper**
- **½ cup bone broth**

1. Preheat the oven to 425 F.
2. Heat a skillet to medium-high heat and add the coconut oil.
3. Pat the chicken thighs with a paper towel to remove excess moisture and set aside. Mix the ghee, garlic, salt and pepper together in a bowl and place the mixture under the skin of the chicken and on the outside.
4. Place the chicken thighs in the pan skin down and sear for 5 minutes, or until browned.
5. Flip the chicken over and add the bone broth around the chicken — do not pour on top of the skin.
6. Place the skillet in the oven and roast the chicken for about 15 minutes, or until the chicken reaches an internal temperature of 165 F.
7. Let the chicken rest for 3–4 minutes and then serve.

COCONUT CRUSTED CHICKEN TENDERS

Serving Size: 2   Time: 35 minutes

- ¼ cup coconut oil
- ⅛ cup each: coconut flour and coconut flakes
- ½ teaspoon each: ground turmeric, garlic powder, sea salt and black pepper
- 6 chicken tenderloins

1. Preheat the oven to 425 F.
2. Melt the coconut oil in a small pot, then pour into a medium bowl and set aside. In a separate medium bowl, mix the coconut flour, flakes and all spices together until well combined.
3. Dip each tenderloin in the coconut oil, coating evenly, and then dip into the coconut flour mixture, coating evenly. Place the tenderloins on a large baking sheet lined with parchment paper and bake for 15 minutes.
4. Flip each tenderloin and continue baking for an additional 15 minutes, or until golden brown. Allow to cool for 2–3 minutes and serve.

BEEF HASH

WITH SQUASH, ONION AND GARLIC

Serving Size: 4   Time: 25 minutes

- 1 pound lean grass-fed ground beef
- 1 cup diced red onion
- 2 cups chopped zucchini
- 2 cups chopped yellow squash
- 2 large garlic cloves, minced
- 1 teaspoon each: sea salt and black pepper

1. Heat a skillet to medium-high heat, add the beef and break into small pieces.
2. Add the onion, zucchini, squash, garlic, salt and pepper. Cook for 8–10 minutes, or until the beef is cooked through and the vegetables are tender.

Coconut Crusted Chicken Tenders

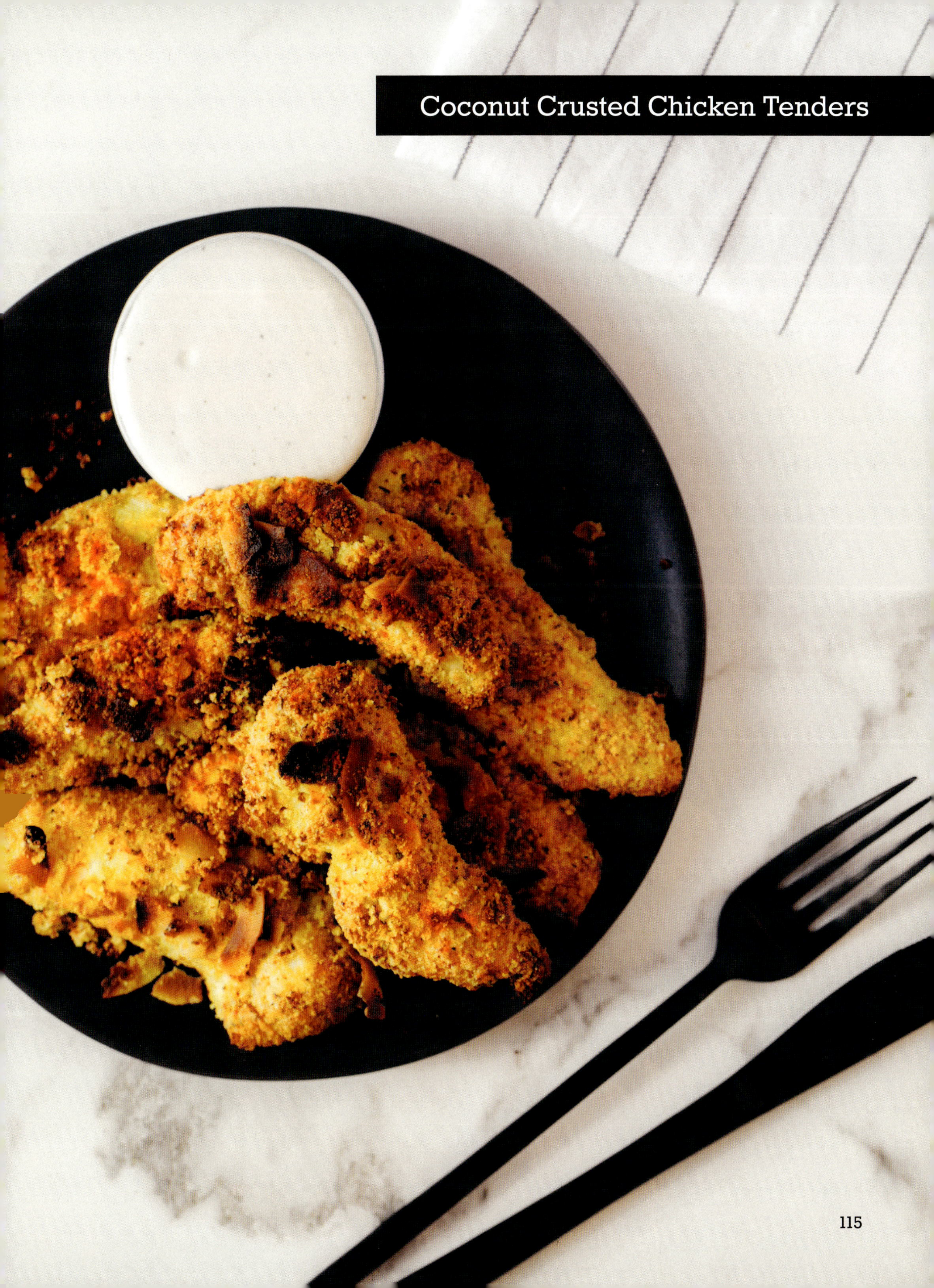

FLATBREAD PIZZA

Serving Size: 1 pizza crust   **Time:** 25–30 minutes

- 1 cup arrowroot starch
- ⅓ cup coconut flour
- ¼ teaspoon sea salt
- ½ cup full-fat coconut milk
- ¼ cup unsalted grass-fed butter
- ¼ cup water
- 2 cloves garlic, smashed and minced
- 1 egg
- Topping ingredients (tomato sauce, goat cheese, asparagus, olives, artichoke hearts, peppers, etc.)

1. Place a pizza stone in the oven and heat to 450 F.
2. Whisk together the arrowroot starch, coconut flour and salt in a medium bowl.
3. Next, heat the coconut milk, butter, water and garlic in a small pot over medium heat. Remove from the heat just as it simmers.
4. Add the hot liquid ingredients to the dry ingredients and mix to combine. Allow the mixture to cool slightly.
5. Whisk the egg in a small bowl. Add the egg to the batter and mix well. Allow the mixture to sit for 5 minutes.
6. Spread the dough in a thin layer on parchment paper the size of the pizza stone. Carefully transfer the dough to the hot pizza stone.
7. Bake for 5–7 minutes, then remove and add your favorite toppings.
8. Place back in the oven and bake for 10–15 minutes, or until golden-brown.

BAKED CHICKEN

WITH GINGERED CARROTS

Serving Size: 4   Time: 2 hours 45 minutes

Chicken:
- ¼ cup ghee
- ¼ cup olive oil
- 2 teaspoons each: sea salt and black pepper
- 2 cloves garlic, smashed and minced
- 4½ pound whole chicken

Gingered Carrots:
- ½ tablespoon olive oil
- 1 teaspoon each: turmeric, ground ginger, lemon zest, sea salt and black pepper
- ½-inch piece fresh ginger, peeled and grated
- 8 carrots, chopped

1. Preheat the oven to 300 F.
2. Combine the ghee, olive oil, salt, pepper and garlic in a bowl. Mix until well combined. Truss the chicken and gently coat with the ghee mixture. Sprinkle on more salt and pepper if desired. Place the chicken in a casserole dish and roast for 2½ hours.
3. While the chicken is baking, take a medium bowl and add the olive oil, turmeric, ground ginger, fresh ginger, lemon zest, salt and pepper. Mix well. Toss the carrots in the mixture until evenly coated.
4. When the chicken has 1 hour left, add the carrots and olive oil mixture to the casserole dish and bake together for the remaining hour. Allow the chicken and carrots to cool for 10 minutes before serving.

CITRUS AND GARLIC ROASTED CHICKEN

Serving Size: 4   Time: 2 hours

- ⅓ cup ghee
- 2 tablespoons minced garlic
- 2 limes, zest and sliced
- 3 lemons, zest and sliced
- 2 teaspoons sea salt
- 1 teaspoon black pepper
- 4½ pound whole chicken

1. Preheat the oven to 300 F.
2. Combine the ghee, garlic, lime zest, lemon zest, salt and pepper in bowl and mix into a paste.
3. Take 1-2 tablespoons of the ghee mixture and rub it under the chicken skin. Then add several of the citrus slices inside the chicken cavity.
4. Truss the chicken with some butcher's twine, and then rub the rest of the ghee mixture all over the chicken.
5. Place the chicken in a large cast iron pan and roast for approximately 2½ hours, or until the internal temperature reaches 165 F.
6. Let the roasted chicken set for about 15 minutes and then serve.

CHICKEN MARSALA

Serving Size: 4   Time: 30 minutes

- **3 tablespoons coconut flour**
- **2 tablespoons almond flour**
- **1 teaspoon each: garlic powder, sea salt, black pepper and dried oregano**
- **4 boneless, skinless chicken breasts**
- **3 tablespoons ghee**
- **1 cup sliced mushrooms**
- **½ cup marsala wine**

1. Mix the flours, garlic powder, salt, pepper and oregano in a medium bowl or shallow pan.
2. Pat the chicken breasts dry, then coat the chicken breasts in the flour mixture.
3. Heat a skillet over medium-high heat and add the ghee and then the chicken breasts. Cook the chicken until slightly browned on one side.
4. Flip the chicken breasts and add the mushrooms to the skillet. Cook for another 2–3 minutes.
5. Pour the marsala wine over the chicken and cover the skillet. Reduce the heat to low and allow to simmer for 15 minutes, or until the chicken is cooked through.

PALEO MEATLOAF

Serving Size: 4   Time: 1 hour 10 minutes

- **3 tablespoons coconut flour**
- **2 tablespoons almond flour**
- **½ teaspoon each: sea salt and black pepper**
- **1 teaspoon each: cayenne pepper, thyme and cumin**
- **1½ pounds grass-fed ground beef**
- **1 egg**
- **1 medium-sized onion, chopped**
- **2 cloves garlic, minced**
- **½ cup organic ketchup**
- **1 tablespoon maple syrup**

1. Preheat the oven to 350 F.
2. Mix the flours, salt, pepper, cayenne, thyme and cumin in a high-speed blender until fine.
3. Combine the mixture with the remaining ingredients in a mixing bowl.
4. Transfer to a greased loaf pan and pack lightly.
5. Bake for 1 hour, or until cooked through.

GAME DAY BBQ CHICKEN TENDERS

Serving Size: 2   Time: 20 minutes

- 1 pound chicken tender strips
- ½ cup cassava flour
- ½ teaspoon paprika
- ¼ teaspoon each: cayenne pepper, sea salt, black pepper and garlic powder
- 2 tablespoons coconut oil
- ½ cup hot sauce
- ¼ cup ghee

1. Cut all chicken strips in half.
2. Combine the flour, paprika, cayenne, salt, pepper and garlic powder in a medium-sized bowl.
3. Pour in hot sauce in a separate bowl.
4. Melt the coconut oil in a pan over medium heat.
5. Coat both sides of the chicken with the flour mixture.
6. Dip the floured chicken in the hot sauce.
7. Place all of the chicken in the pan and cook for 6–7 minutes.
8. Add the ghee to the pan and flip the chicken.
9. Cook the second side for 6–7 minutes, or until cooked through (reaches 165 F internally).
10. Remove from the heat and add additional hot sauce as needed.
11. Pair with the Honey Mustard Dressing (page 101).

COCONUT CURRIED TURKEY SOUP

SERVED OVER CAULIFLOWER RICE

Serving Size: 4–6   Time: 1 hour 10 minutes

- 1 medium head cauliflower, chopped
- 2 tablespoons coconut oil or ghee
- 3 carrots, peeled and sliced
- 3 cups chopped cabbage
- 1 tablespoon ground turmeric
- ½ tablespoon each: garam masala, ground ginger and cinnamon
- ¼ cup full-fat coconut milk
- 6–8 cups bone broth or vegetable broth
- 2–3 cups cooked and chopped turkey
- Sea salt and black pepper to taste
- 2–4 tablespoons toasted pumpkin seeds

1. Process the cauliflower in a food processor until rice-like. Set aside.
2. Melt the coconut oil or ghee in a large pot over medium heat. Add the carrots and cabbage, stirring continuously for about 10 minutes. Add the spices and continue to cook for about 5 minutes, until the aromas are released. Pour in the coconut milk, stirring until evenly mixed, then add in the broth and turkey. Bring the mixture to a boil.
3. Reduce the heat and simmer for about 50 minutes. Let cool for 5 minutes. Add the salt and pepper to taste. Serve in a bowl over the cauliflower rice, garnished with the toasted pumpkin seeds.

MEATBALLS

Serving Size: 4   Time: 45 minutes

- **1 pound ground grass-fed beef**
- **2 eggs, whisked**
- **One 10-ounce package frozen spinach, thawed and drained**
- **¼ cup finely grated raw sheep milk cheese, such as Pecorino or Zamorano**
- **¼ teaspoon sea salt**
- **½ teaspoon cracked black pepper**
- **1 tablespoon olive oil**

1. Place all of the ingredients except the oil in a bowl. Mix together and form into 1 to 1½-inch meatballs.
2. Heat the oil in a 10-inch skillet over medium-high heat. Brown the meatballs well on all sides in the skillet and place on paper towels to cool briefly before serving.

SPAGHETTI SQUASH

WITH ROASTED CHICKEN, LEMON AND PARSLEY

Serving Size: 4	Time: 1 hour

- **1 medium spaghetti squash**
- **2 tablespoons ghee (divided)**
- **1½ pounds chicken thighs, skin on and bone in**
- **¼ teaspoon each: sea salt and black pepper**
- **2 tablespoons chopped garlic**
- **Juice of 1 lemon**
- **½ cup chicken broth**
- **¼ cup chopped parsley (divided)**

1. Preheat the oven to 425 F. Cut the spaghetti squash in half and scoop out the seeds. Place the squash face down and cook for 40–50 minutes, or until the squash is soft.
2. Set aside and let cool some, and then use a fork to scrape the spaghetti out.
3. Heat 1 tablespoon of the ghee in a large skillet over medium-high heat and sprinkle the outside of the chicken with the salt and pepper.
4. Add the chicken to the pan skin side down, sear for 5 minutes and then remove the chicken and set on a plate.
5. Add the garlic to the skillet and brown it for about 30 seconds. Then add the lemon juice, broth and 1 tablespoon of the parsley and stir.
6. Add the chicken back to the pan, skin side up, and roast in the oven for 10–12 minutes, or until the internal chicken temperature reaches 165 F.
7. Toss some of the hot spaghetti squash with the remaining ghee. Divide the spaghetti squash onto four plates and top with the chicken and more parsley and serve.

BISON BURGER CHARD WRAPS

WITH KIMCHI

Serving Size: 4   Time: 25 minutes

- 1 pound ground bison
- 1 teaspoon each: sea salt and black pepper
- 2 garlic cloves, chopped
- 2 large Swiss chard leaves
- ½ cup kimchi (divided)

1. Mix the bison, salt, pepper and garlic in a large bowl and form four large patties.
2. Heat a skillet over medium-high heat, add the burger patties and sear about 5–6 minutes on each side, or until the internal temperature reaches between 155–165 F.
3. While the burgers are cooking, take a pairing knife and carefully cut the stem out of the chard leaves. Divide the four leaves onto a large plate.
4. Once the burgers are done cooking, place a burger in the middle of each chard leaf and top with the kimchi. Carefully wrap each leaf around each burger and serve immediately.

LAMB BURGER OVER MASSAGED KALE SALAD

Serving Size: 4   Time: 40–45 minutes

Dressing:
- 5–6 tablespoons Cauliflower Hummus (page 153)
- 1 tablespoon apple cider vinegar
- 1 teaspoon lemon juice

Lamb Burger:
- ½ medium red onion, sliced
- 1 clove garlic, peeled
- ½ pound minced lean lamb
- ½ pound lean ground beef
- 1 teaspoon each: Himalayan salt and black pepper
- ½ teaspoon coconut oil
- 1 cup kimchi or sauerkraut (divided)
- avocado slices

Salad:
- 4 cups chopped kale, stems removed
- 1 tablespoon each: olive oil and lemon juice
- ½ teaspoon sea salt
- ¼ teaspoon black pepper

1. Mix the Cauliflower Hummus, apple cider vinegar and lemon juice in a small bowl. Cover and refrigerate.
2. Combine the onion and garlic in a food processor and pulse until finely chopped.
3. Transfer the mixture to a large mixing bowl along with the lamb, ground beef and spices, using your hands to combine all the ingredients. Form 4 patties.
4. Chill in the refrigerator for 15–20 minutes to firm.
5. Melt the coconut oil in a large nonstick skillet over medium-high heat. Fry the burgers for 7–8 minutes per side, or until the internal temperature reaches between 155–165 F. Set aside the kimchi or sauerkraut and avocado slices.
6. While the burgers are cooking, add the kale to a large bowl and combine with the oil, lemon juice, salt and pepper. Massage the ingredients together.
7. Serve the burgers over a bed of the massaged kale. Top with the sauerkraut or kimchi, dressing, and avocado slices.

LAMB-STUFFED CABBAGE ROLLS

Serving Size: 10   Time: 2 hours 45 minutes

Lamb Mixture:
- **1 pound minced lean lamb**
- **1 cup long-grain rice, soaked for 20 minutes**
- **1 tablespoon Himalayan salt**
- **1 teaspoon each: cumin, chili powder and dried oregano**
- **½ teaspoon each: smoked paprika and cinnamon**

Vegetable Mixture:
- **2 tablespoons extra virgin olive oil**
- **3 tablespoons unsalted grass-fed butter**
- **1 teaspoon Himalayan salt**
- **1 teaspoon black pepper**
- **½ white onion, diced**
- **2 cloves garlic, crushed and minced**
- **1 red bell pepper, diced**
- **1 jalapeño, seeded and diced**
- **1 teaspoon each: cumin, chili powder and cinnamon**
- **1 head of cabbage, cored**
- **1 tablespoon freshly squeezed lime juice (about 1/4 small lime)**
- **Sea salt and black pepper to taste**

Sauce Mixture:
- **One 28-ounce can fire-roasted whole tomatoes**
- **2 tablespoons tomato paste**
- **2 Roma tomatoes, diced**
- **½ white onion, diced**

1. Use your hands to mix together the lamb, rice and spices in a large mixing bowl. Set aside.
2. Stir the oil, butter, salt and pepper together in a medium saucepan over medium heat until the butter is melted. Add the onion, garlic, bell pepper and jalapeño.
3. Cook for 5–8 minutes, stirring occasionally to soften the vegetables. Add the spices, mix well and remove from the heat. Allow the mixture to cool to room temperature while you prepare the cabbage leaves.
4. Fill a large stockpot halfway full with water and bring to a boil. Pull the head of cabbage apart. Add a generous dash of salt and the cabbage leaves to the boiling water and boil for 2–3 minutes.
5. Drain the leaves and allow to cool. Once cooled, trim the spine of each cabbage leaf with a paring knife to promote easy rolling.
6. Stir the lime juice into the vegetable mixture. Add the vegetables to the lamb mixture and mix well with your hands. Cover and refrigerate while preparing the sauce.
7. Heat the oven to 350 F.
8. Bring the fire-roasted tomatoes, tomato paste, Roma tomatoes and onion to a boil in a medium saucepan. Boil for 5 minutes, stirring occasionally. Reduce the heat and simmer until the tomatoes break apart easily with a spoon, about 7 minutes. Remove from the heat and set aside.
9. Line the bottom of a 9 x 13-inch casserole dish with 6 small cabbage leaves.

10. Remove the lamb mixture from the refrigerator. Lay 1 cabbage leaf flat with the stem pointing toward you. Add ½ cup of the lamb mixture to the bottom edge of the cabbage leaf. Pull the bottom edge of the cabbage leaf up and over the lamb, forming a log.

11. Tightly roll the log to the end of the cabbage leaf. Place the roll in the casserole dish seam side down. Repeat with the remaining lamb and cabbage leaves, making 2 rows of 5 rolls each.

12. Sprinkle the rolls with the salt and pepper. Spoon the tomato sauce over the top of the rolls and cover with the remaining cabbage leaves.

13. Bake for 90 minutes. Allow the cabbage rolls to rest for 20 minutes before serving.

SHEPHERD'S PIE

Serving Size: 8–10   Time: 1 hour 15 minutes

Filling:
- 2 tablespoons coconut oil
- 1 pound grass-fed ground beef or lamb
- 2 large carrots, sliced thin
- 1 yellow onion, diced
- 1½ cups green frozen peas, cooked according to package directions

Gravy:
- 2 cups beef or lamb stock
- 1 cup chopped cauliflower
- 1 onion, chopped
- ½ teaspoon each: sea salt and black pepper
- 2 teaspoons each: fresh minced thyme and fresh minced rosemary
- 3 cloves pressed or minced garlic
- 1½ teaspoons Worcestershire sauce
- 4 tablespoons unsalted grass-fed butter
- ½ cup arrowroot starch

Topping:
- Mashed Caul-Tatoes (page 86)

Filling:

1. Heat the coconut oil in a large skillet over medium-high heat. Add the meat, carrots, and onion and cook, stirring often, until the meat is browned and the vegetables have begun to soften, 10–15 minutes.
2. Remove from the heat and drain the filling mixture to remove excess fat. Add the peas, stirring to combine. Pour the filling in the bottom of an 8 x 8 baking dish and set aside.
3. Preheat the oven to 400 F.

Gravy:

1. Combine the stock, cauliflower, onion, salt and pepper in a medium pot. Heat, uncovered, over medium-high heat until simmering. Simmer 10 minutes. Add the thyme, rosemary and garlic and remove from the heat.
2. Place the Worcestershire and butter in a high-speed blender and pour the stock mixture over top. Purée together until smooth. Add the arrowroot starch and purée until smooth.
3. Pour the gravy evenly over the filling in the dish. Spread the Mashed Caul-Tatoes on top.
4. Bake at 400 F for 30 minutes, or until the topping begins to brown and the gravy is bubbling. Cool for 10 minutes before serving.

WHITE CHICKEN CHILI

Serving Size: 6–8   Time: 1 hour 15 minutes

- 3 boneless skinless chicken breasts, at room temperature
- 4 tablespoons coconut oil, melted (divided)
- 2 small yellow onions, diced
- ¼ red onion, diced
- 1 red bell pepper, diced
- 1 jalapeño pepper, seeded and diced
- 2 cloves garlic, peeled and diced
- 2 teaspoons each: cumin and chili powder
- 1 teaspoon smoked paprika
- 2 cups chicken broth
- One 28-ounce can whole, peeled, fire-roasted tomatoes with juice
- One 14-ounce can cannellini beans, drained and rinsed
- Sea salt and black pepper to taste
- Lime wedge and cilantro (garnish)

1. Heat the oven to 425 F. Line a baking sheet with parchment paper.
2. Rub the chicken breasts with 2 tablespoons of the coconut oil and season with salt and pepper. Place on the lined baking sheet and bake for 25 minutes. While the chicken is baking, prepare the soup.
3. Heat the remaining 2 tablespoons of coconut oil in a large soup pot over medium-high heat until the oil shimmers. Add the onions, bell pepper, jalapeño, garlic, cumin, chili powder and paprika. Cook for 8 minutes, stirring frequently, until the onions are soft.
4. Stir in the chicken stock and fire-roasted tomatoes. Increase the heat to high and bring the mixture to a boil. Boil for 2 minutes. Reduce the heat to low, cover and simmer for 35 minutes.
5. Remove the chicken from the oven and allow it to cool slightly. Using two forks, pull apart the chicken into bite-size pieces.
6. With a wooden spoon, break apart the tomatoes in the chili. Stir in the beans and the chicken. Cover and simmer for 20 more minutes.
7. Allow the soup to rest for 10 minutes. Add more salt and pepper to taste. Serve topped with the lime wedge, cilantro or both.

137

SEARED AHI TUNA STIR-FRY

Serving Size: 6   Time: 20 minutes

- 6 tablespoons olive oil (divided)
- 1 medium green cabbage, cored and chopped
- 3 cups sliced shiitake mushrooms
- 2 baby bok choy, thinly sliced
- 2 carrots, peeled and julienned
- 4 tablespoons Bragg's liquid aminos (divided)
- 2 cups chicken bone broth
- 4 tablespoons ghee
- 2 tablespoons apple cider vinegar (divided)
- ½ teaspoon sea salt
- Three 5-ounce ahi tuna steaks
- Sea salt and black pepper to taste

1. Heat 3 tablespoons of the olive oil in a large, heavy skillet over medium-high heat.
2. Add the cabbage, mushrooms, bok choy and carrots and stir-fry until the vegetables are crisp-tender, about 3–4 minutes. Gently stir in the liquid aminos. Transfer the mixture to a medium bowl.
3. In the same skillet, add the bone broth, a dash of the olive oil, remaining liquid aminos, ghee, apple cider vinegar and salt. Stirring continuously, boil for about 2–3 minutes. Keep warm.
4. Season the tuna steaks with the salt and pepper.
5. Heat the remaining olive oil in a large skillet over high heat.
6. Add the tuna steaks and cook to desired doneness, about 2 minutes per side for medium-rare.
7. Plate the vegetables, top with the tuna and ladle the sauce over. Serve immediately.

BEEF SHORT RIBS

Serving Size: 4	Time: 3 hours 15 minutes

- **4 pounds beef short ribs, cut into 3-inch pieces**
- **Sea salt and black pepper to taste**
- **½ cup coconut sugar**
- **1 teaspoon paprika**
- **½ teaspoon each: garlic powder and thyme**
- **1 tablespoon each: apple cider vinegar and Dijon mustard**
- **3 tablespoons organic Worcestershire sauce**
- **⅔ cup organic ketchup**

1. Preheat the oven to 300 F.
2. Place the ribs in a 9 x 13 pan and season with the salt and pepper to taste.
3. Combine the remaining ingredients in a separate bowl.
4. Pour the sauce over the ribs and mix well to coat all the pieces.
5. Cover with foil and roast for about 3 hours, or until cooked through.
6. During last 20 minutes of cooking, remove the foil to brown the top of the ribs.

STIR-FRY SALMON

Serving Size: 2　　　　Time: 20 minutes

- ¼ cup coconut aminos
- 2 teaspoons each: rice vinegar and sesame oil
- 1 cup chopped bell peppers
- 1 onion, chopped
- 1 pound wild-caught Alaskan salmon, skinned and cut into 1½-inch cubes
- 1 tablespoon each: coconut oil, finely chopped fresh ginger and sesame seeds
- 4 garlic cloves, finely chopped
- 1½ cups chopped mushrooms
- 1 head broccoli, chopped and blanched

1. Add the coconut aminos, vinegar, sesame oil, peppers and onions in a large skillet over medium heat. Cook the peppers and onions until translucent.
2. Add the salmon to the pan and coat it with the mixture.
3. Add the coconut oil, ginger, sesame seeds, garlic, mushrooms and broccoli.
4. Continue to cook until the salmon is cooked through and then serve.

CHICKEN POT PIE

Serving Size: 4–6   Time: 2 hours

Almond Flour Pie Crust:
- 1 cup almond flour
- ¼ cup arrowroot starch
- ½ teaspoon each: baking powder and sea salt
- 6 tablespoons unsalted grass-fed butter, cubed and very cold
- ½ cup cold water
- Juice of ½ lemon, chilled

Filling:
- Unsalted grass-fed butter or coconut oil, for greasing
- 2 cups cooked pulled chicken
- ½ cup each: chopped turnip, chopped carrot and chopped celery

Chicken Gravy:
- 2 cups chicken stock
- 1 cup chopped cauliflower
- 1 medium yellow onion, chopped
- 1½ teaspoons each: fresh sage, fresh thyme, sea salt and pressed or minced garlic
- 4 tablespoons unsalted grass-fed butter
- 3 tablespoons arrowroot starch

Pie Crust:

1. Whisk together the dry ingredients in a large mixing bowl until well combined. Transfer the dry ingredients to a food processor. Add the cold butter and process until the butter is the size of peas.

2. Combine the cold water and cold lemon juice in a small bowl. Add a small amount of the water and lemon juice to the food processor and process. Continue adding the water and lemon juice and process just until the dough comes together.

3. Remove the dough and form it into a ball. Wrap the dough in a sheet of wax paper, place it in an airtight container, and refrigerate for 15 minutes. Prepare the filling while the dough chills.

Finishing the Crust:

1. Remove the chilled dough from the refrigerator and place between 2 sheets of wax paper. Flatten the dough with your hands, and then with a rolling pin, roll the dough into a 10-inch circle.

2. Return the dough, in the wax paper, to the refrigerator.

3. Heat the oven to 400 F.

Filling:

1. Grease a deep-dish pie pan with butter or coconut oil.

2. Mix together the pulled chicken, turnip, carrots and celery in a large bowl.

3. Spread the chicken and vegetables in the pie pan. Set aside.

Gravy:

1. Combine the chicken stock, cauliflower, onion, herbs, garlic and salt in a medium pot. Cover and cook over medium-high heat until simmering. Simmer for 8 minutes. Remove from the heat.
2. Place the butter in a high-speed blender, add the stock and vegetable mixture, and purée until very smooth. Return the puréed mixture to the pot and heat on medium until simmering.
3. Whisk the arrowroot starch with 3 tablespoons of the pureed mixture until smooth, add to the pot and stir constantly until slightly thickened. Remove from the heat.

Assembling the Pie:

1. Retrieve the dough from the refrigerator, peel off the wax paper and place on top of the pie.
2. Press the edges of the crust into to the pie pan. Cut small vents in the center of the crust.
3. Bake the pie for 45–50 minutes, or until the crust is golden brown and the sauce is bubbling. Allow to cool for 15 minutes before serving.

CHAPTER 5

Snacks and Appetizers

BANANA BREAD

Serving Size: 6–8   Time: 55 minutes

- **4 eggs**
- **3 medium overly ripe bananas, mashed**
- **¼ cup raw honey**
- **¼ cup full-fat coconut milk**
- **1 tablespoon vanilla extract**
- **1 teaspoon baking powder**
- **2¼ cups almond flour**
- **½ teaspoon each: sea salt and cinnamon**

1. Preheat the oven to 350 F.
2. Mix the eggs, bananas, honey, coconut milk and vanilla in a bowl.
3. Combine the remaining ingredients in a separate bowl.
4. Combine both mixtures and stir until well incorporated.
5. Grease a bread pan and pour in the batter. Bake for 35–50 minutes.

NO-BAKE BONE BROTH PROTEIN BAR

Serving Size: 12   Time: 1 hour 10 minutes

- **4 cups cashews**
- **3 cups Medjool dates, pitted**
- **2 tablespoons cashew butter**
- **2 teaspoons each: vanilla extract and cinnamon**
- **4 tablespoons bone broth protein powder**
- **2 tablespoons water**
- **Dash of sea salt (about 1/8 teaspoon)**

1. Pulse the cashews in a food processor until small chunks are formed. Add in all other ingredients and blend on high until the dough is formed, scraping the sides as needed.
2. Evenly distribute the mixture in a cupcake pan, filled with liners.
3. Cover and freeze for 1 hour before serving.

Banana Bread

Pumpkin Bread

CHOCOLATE CHIP ZUCCHINI BREAD

Serving Size: 8   Time: 1 hour

- **2 cups grated zucchini**
- **¾ cup almond flour**
- **1 cup cassava flour**
- **½ cup each: gluten-free oat flour and coconut sugar**
- **¾–1 cup organic dark chocolate chips**
- **1 teaspoon vanilla extract**
- **½ teaspoon each: baking soda and baking powder**
- **¼ cup coconut oil, melted**
- **3 eggs**
- **Dash of sea salt**

1. Preheat the oven to 300 F.
2. Line a loaf pan with parchment paper. Set aside.
3. Line a large bowl with a cheese cloth, allowing the cloth to fall over the sides.
4. Grate the zucchini into the cheese cloth.
5. Wrap the zucchini in the cloth and squeeze any excess water out into the bowl.
6. Add the flours, sugar and chocolate chips in a large bowl. Whisk until well incorporated and set aside.
7. Whisk the remaining ingredients (including the zucchini) until well combined. Then add to the dry ingredients, mixing evenly.
8. Pour the mixture into the pan and bake for 35–45 minutes. Let stand for 10 minutes and serve.

PUMPKIN BREAD

Serving Size: 8–10   Time: 1 hour 25 minutes

- **1 cup almond flour**
- **¼ cup coconut flour**
- **½ teaspoon each: sea salt, baking powder and pumpkin pie spice**
- **1 teaspoon cinnamon**
- **¾ cup canned pumpkin**
- **¼ cup maple syrup**
- **¼ cup coconut oil**
- **3–4 eggs**

1. Preheat the oven to 325 F.
2. Combine all dry ingredients in a bowl.
3. Combine all wet ingredients (the last 4) in another bowl.
4. Mix both bowls together until well incorporated.
5. Pour into a greased loaf pan and bake for 45–60 minutes.

BLUEBERRY MUFFINS

Serving Size: 12   Time: 40 minutes

- 1 cup gluten-free oat flour
- ½ cup almond flour
- ½ teaspoon baking powder
- ¼ teaspoon sea salt
- 3 eggs
- ½ cup each: raw honey and applesauce
- 1 teaspoon each: vanilla extract and apple cider vinegar
- ⅛ cup coconut oil, melted
- 1 cup fresh or frozen blueberries

1. Preheat the oven to 350 F.
2. Line a standard muffin tin with liners and set aside.
3. Whisk the oat flour, almond flour, baking powder, and salt in a large mixing bowl.
4. Combine the eggs, honey, applesauce, vanilla extract, apple cider vinegar and coconut oil in a separate bowl and stir until well combined.
5. Slowly add the dry mixture to the wet mixture and stir well.
6. Fold in the blueberries into the batter.
7. Bake for 25–35 minutes, or until golden brown on top.

Cauliflower Hummus

CAULIFLOWER HUMMUS

Serving Size: 4   Time: 1 hour

- **1 medium-sized cauliflower**
- **½ cup tahini**
- **2 tablespoons olive oil**
- **2 large garlic cloves**
- **⅓ cup lemon juice**
- **1 teaspoon sea salt**
- **½ teaspoon black pepper**
- **¼ cup chopped parsley (garnish)**
- **1 tablespoon olive oil (garnish)**

1. Preheat the oven to 425 F and line a baking sheet with parchment paper.
2. Remove the florets from the cauliflower and add them to the baking sheet. Toss in a small amount of olive oil and roast for 15 minutes.
3. Add the roasted cauliflower to a food processor with the tahini, olive oil, garlic, lemon juice, salt and pepper and purée until smooth.
4. Pour the hummus into an airtight container and place in the refrigerator until cold.
5. Serve in a bowl and top with the parsley and olive oil if desired.

COFFEE CAKE

Serving Size: 9   Time: 35 minutes

- **2 tablespoons coconut oil**
- **1 egg**
- **1 teaspoon vanilla extract**
- **¼ cup raw honey**
- **1½ cups almond flour**
- **1 teaspoon cinnamon**
- **2 teaspoons baking powder**
- **½ teaspoon sea salt**
- **½ cup full-fat coconut milk**
- **½ cup almond flour (topping)**
- **1½ tablespoons coconut oil (topping)**
- **1 tablespoon raw honey (topping)**
- **2 teaspoons cinnamon (topping)**

1. Preheat the oven to 350 F.
2. Stir the coconut oil, egg, vanilla and honey together in a bowl.
3. Combine the almond flour, cinnamon, baking powder and salt in a small bowl.
4. Add the dry ingredients to the wet ingredients, along with the coconut milk, and stir until smooth.
5. Pour into an 8 × 8 baking pan.
6. In a small bowl, mix the almond flour, coconut oil, honey and cinnamon for topping.
7. Spread the topping over the cake.
8. Bake for 20–25 minutes.

SWEET POTATO HUMMUS

Serving Size: 6   **Time: 2 hours**

- 4 medium sweet potatoes
- ½ cup tahini
- 2 tablespoons olive oil
- 2 large garlic cloves
- 2 tablespoons lemon juice
- ¼ teaspoon cumin
- 1 teaspoon sea salt
- ½ teaspoon black pepper
- 1 tablespoon olive oil (garnish)
- ¼ cup chopped fresh cilantro (garnish)

1. Chop the sweet potatoes into large chunks and add to a pot of boiling water.
2. Let the potatoes boil for 30–40 minutes, or until they are soft.
3. Drain the water and sweet potatoes through a sieve and carefully peel the skins off of the sweet potatoes.
4. Add the sweet potatoes to a food processor along with the tahini, olive oil, garlic, lemon juice, cumin, salt and pepper. Purée until smooth.
5. Refrigerate the hummus in an airtight container until cooled and then garnish with the olive oil and cilantro before serving.

APPLE CHIPS

Serving Size: 4   Time: 50 minutes

- **6 large apples**
- **1 teaspoon each: cinnamon, ground ginger and nutmeg**

1. Preheat the oven to 200 F.
2. Core the apples and then slice thinly with a knife or mandoline.
3. Toss the apples with the spices and place on a baking sheet lined with parchment paper.
4. Bake for 1 hour.
5. Sprinkle with additional cinnamon, if desired.

GUACAMOLE

Serving Size: 4–6   Time: 10 minutes

- **2 avocados**
- **Juice of 1 lime**
- **2 cloves of garlic, minced**
- **1 tomato, chopped or ¼ cup salsa**
- **1 teaspoon sea salt**
- **Pinch of black pepper**
- **½ teaspoon fresh cilantro**

1. Spoon out the avocados into a large bowl. Add the lime juice, garlic and tomato or salsa.
2. With a spoon, mash together until the mixture becomes creamy.
3. Add the salt, pepper and cilantro. Refrigerate and serve with Apple Chips (see above recipe).

KALE CHIPS

Serving Size: 2   Time: 15 minutes

- **1 bunch kale, chopped**
- **2 tablespoons coconut oil**
- **1 tablespoon lemon juice**
- **¼ teaspoon sea salt**

1. Preheat the oven to 350 F.
2. Chop the kale into ½-inch pieces.
3. Place all ingredients in a large bowl and massage the oil, lemon juice and salt into the kale using your hands.
4. Place on parchment lined baking sheets and bake for 12 minutes.

SPINACH AND GOAT CHEESE STUFFED MUSHROOMS

Serving Size: 8 mushrooms   Time: 25 minutes

- **8 large portobello mushroom caps**
- **1 tablespoon olive oil (divided)**
- **6 cups spinach**
- **1 teaspoon minced garlic**
- **1 tablespoon sea salt**
- **1 tablespoon black pepper**
- **½ cup goat cheese crumbles**

1. Preheat the oven to 400 F.
2. Brush the mushroom caps with ½ tablespoon of the olive oil and place them top down on a baking sheet lined with parchment paper.
3. Bake the mushrooms for 15 minutes.
4. Meanwhile, drizzle the remaining olive oil in a pot over medium-low heat.
5. Add the spinach, garlic, salt and pepper and cook for 5 minutes.
6. Place the spinach and spices in a small bowl and add the goat cheese. Mix well and set aside.
7. Remove the mushrooms from the oven.
8. Flip the mushroom caps and fill them with the spinach and goat cheese mixture. Bake for 5 more minutes. Take out and serve immediately.
9. Sprinkle more goat cheese on top, if desired.

PROTEIN FIG BAR

Serving Size: 4   Time: 4 hours

- 1 cup dried figs
- 1 cup almond butter
- 1 tablespoon flax meal
- 3 tablespoons collagen protein powder
- 2 tablespoons raw honey

1. Line an 8 x 8 baking pan with parchment paper and set aside.
2. Add all ingredients to food processor and blend until the dough starts to form in to a ball.
3. Press the dough evenly into the pan and refrigerate for 3–4 hours, or until the bars set.
4. Cut into squares and store in an airtight container.

CHOCOLATE CHERRY PROTEIN BAR

Serving Size: 4–6   Time: 1 hour 30 minutes

- 1 cup dried cherries
- 5 Medjool dates, pitted
- 1 cup cashew butter
- ½ cup cacao powder
- 3 tablespoons collagen protein powder
- 1 tablespoon flaxseeds
- 2 tablespoons coconut oil
- ½ teaspoon Himalayan salt

1. Line an 8 x 8 baking dish with parchment paper and set aside.
2. Add the dried cherries and dates to a food processor and pulse into small pieces.
3. Add the rest of the ingredients and pulse until it turns into dough.
4. Pour the dough into the baking dish and spread it out evenly.
5. Place the bars in the freezer for 1 hour and then cut into squares.
6. Store in an airtight container in the freezer until ready to be eaten.

Protein Fig Bar

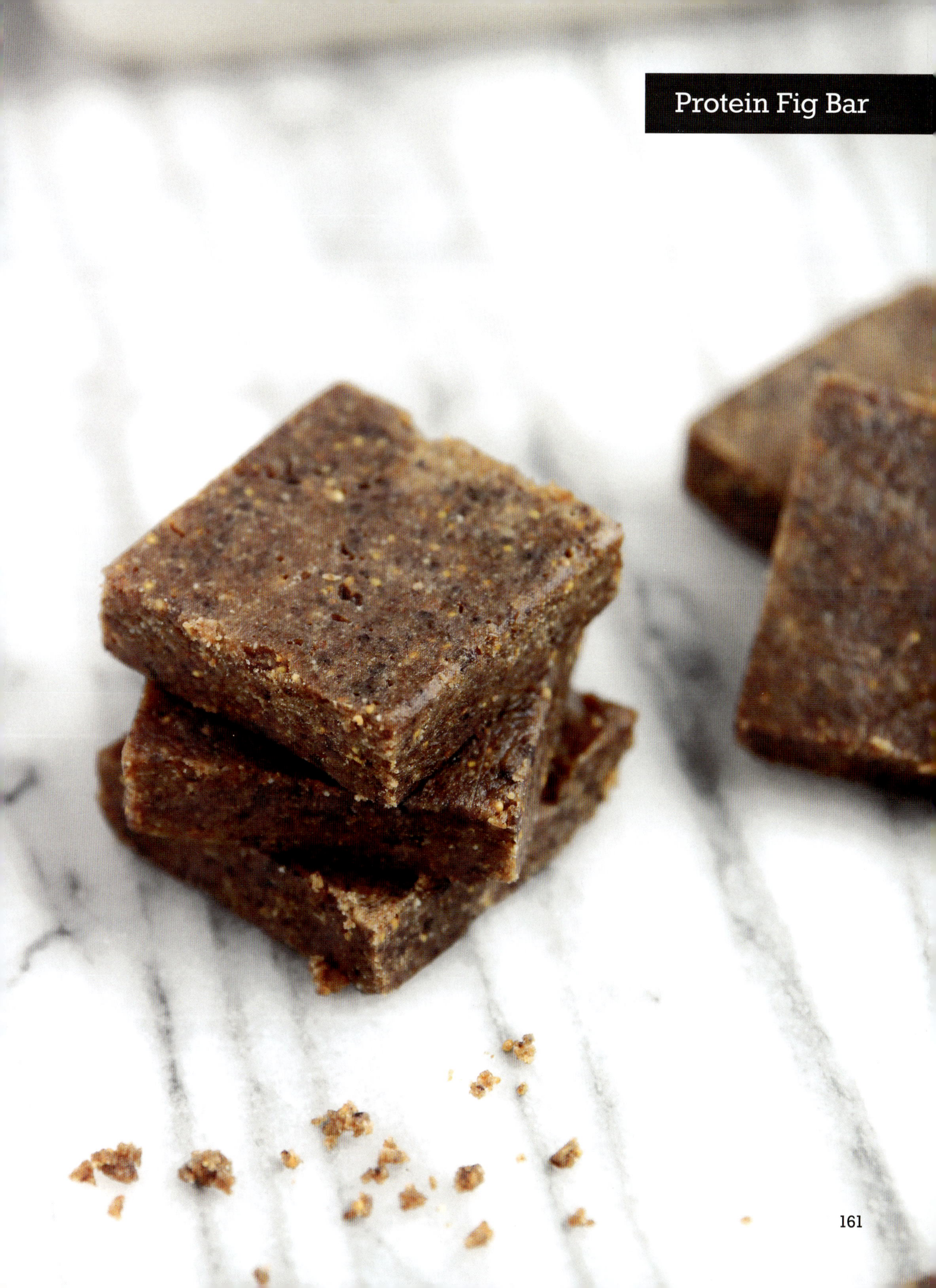

SAUERKRAUT

Serving Size: Makes about 1 gallon   **Time: 20 minutes (4 weeks total)**

- **1 large head of green cabbage, shredded**
- **2 tablespoons sea salt or pickling salt**
- **1 tablespoon caraway seeds**

1. Mix all ingredients in a large bowl. Let stand for 10 minutes.
2. Pack the cabbage mixture into a large glass food container. Top with a lid small enough to fit inside the container and place a sanitized glass jar filled with water on top of the lid to weigh it down.
3. Place in a cool spot overnight. Check to make sure the sauerkraut is completely submerged in liquid. Check the cabbage every other day for 2 weeks, skimming off of any scum that may form on the surface.
4. Let stand for at least 4 weeks total. Then store in airtight container in the refrigerator for up to 6 months.

BLUEBERRY BROTH BAR

Serving Size: 12   Time: 1 hour 10 minutes

- 3 cups macadamia nuts
- 1 cup dried blueberries
- 2 tablespoons coconut butter
- 1 teaspoon vanilla extract
- ¼ teaspoon Himalayan salt
- 3 tablespoons bone broth protein powder
- ¼ teaspoon stevia

1. Process macadamia nuts until small chunks are formed. Process the remaining ingredients until the mixture becomes pasty.
2. Form into bar shapes and refrigerate until firm, approximately 1 hour.

CHAPTER 6

Desserts

APPLE CRISP

Serving Size: 8   Time: 10 minutes

- **8 apples, peeled, cored and chopped**
- **1 cup raisins, soaked and drained**
- **2 teaspoons cinnamon (divided)**
- **¼ teaspoon nutmeg**
- **2 tablespoons lemon juice**
- **2 cups walnuts**
- **1 cup Medjool dates, pitted**
- **⅛ teaspoon sea salt**

1. Preheat the oven to 375 degrees F.
2. Place 2 apples, the raisins, 1 teaspoon of the cinnamon and the nutmeg in a food processor and process until smooth.
3. Toss the remaining chopped apples with the lemon juice in a large bowl. Pour the apple raisin purée over the apples and mix well.
4. Spoon the mixture into 8 mini-tart pans or a large rimmed cookie sheet and set aside.
5. Pulse the walnuts, dates, salt and remaining cinnamon in a food processor until coarsely ground. Be careful not to overmix.
6. Sprinkle the mixture over the apples and press down lightly with your hands.
7. Bake for 30 minutes.

PUMPKIN PIE ICE CREAM

Serving Size: 6–8   Time: 1 hour (total time 3 hours)

- 1 medium butternut squash, peeled, seeded and diced
- Pinch of sea salt
- 1½ cans full-fat coconut milk
  ¾ cup coconut sugar
- 1 teaspoon vanilla extract
- 1 sweet tart apple, cored and
- sliced thick
  ¼ teaspoon each: cinnamon and
- ground ginger
  1 teaspoon pumpkin pie spice
- 2 tablespoons whiskey or bourbon
-

1. Preheat the oven to 425 F.
2. Line a cookie sheet with parchment paper. Spread the squash evenly on the parchment.
3. Sprinkle the squash with the salt and bake for 30 minutes.
4. Meanwhile, make the coconut-caramel syrup. Heat ½ can of the coconut milk in a small pot over medium-high heat. Once hot, add the coconut sugar and simmer at medium heat for 6–8 minutes. Remove from the heat. Add the vanilla, stir and set aside.
5. Remove the squash from the oven. Add the apple to the pan and bake 20 minutes more.
6. Remove the squash and apple from the oven and allow to cool for 10 minutes.
7. In a high-speed blender, combine the remaining can of coconut milk, coconut-caramel syrup, squash, apples, spices and whiskey/bourbon. Purée on high until thoroughly blended and thick.
8. Refrigerate in an airtight container at least 3 hours or overnight. When completely chilled, churn according to manufacturer's instructions.

CHOCOLATE FONDUE

Serving Size: 2   Time: 10 minutes

- ½ cup full-fat coconut milk
- 1 dark chocolate bar, minimum 72% cacao
- Stevia to taste
- Fruit for dipping (strawberries, banana and/or kiwi)

1. Warm the coconut milk in a saucepan over medium heat. Break the chocolate bar into pieces and stir into the coconut milk.
2. Add the stevia until desired sweetness is achieved.
3. Dip the berries or other fruit.

PEPPERMINT PATTIES

Serving Size: 12   Time: 30 minutes

- **2 cups coconut oil, room temperature**
- **½ cup raw honey**
- **1 teaspoon peppermint extract**
- **3 dark chocolate bars, minimum 72% cacao**
- **½ cup coconut oil, melted**

1. Mix the coconut oil, honey and peppermint extract in a bowl.
2. Form patties out of the mixture and place on a plate of parchment paper. Place in the freezer to harden.
3. While waiting, melt the chocolate bars with the ½ cup melted coconut oil in a saucepan over medium-low heat. Remove from the heat and cool for 5–10 minutes.
4. Dip the hardened patties in the chocolate until covered and place back on the plate. Place in the freezer until the chocolate has hardened.

DARK CHOCOLATE COVERED BERRIES

Serving Size: 2–4   Time: 10 minutes

- **2 dark chocolate bars, minimum 72% cacao**
- **2 tablespoons toasted flaxseeds**
- **2 cups fresh blueberries, rinsed and dried**

1. Melt the chocolate in a metal bowl set over a pan of simmering water. Stir frequently until melted and smooth. Stir in the flaxseeds.
2. Remove from the heat.
3. Line a baking sheet with waxed paper.
4. Add the blueberries to the chocolate, and stir gently to coat. Spoon small clumps of blueberries onto the waxed paper. Refrigerate until firm, about 10 minutes. Store in a cool place in an airtight container. These will last about 2 days.

CHOCOLATE CARAMEL BROWNIES

Serving Size: 9   Time: 35 minutes

- ¼ cup coconut flour
- 1¼ cups cacao powder
- ¼ cup coconut sugar
- 1 teaspoon each: sea salt and baking soda
- 4 eggs
- ½ cup raw honey
- 1 tablespoon vanilla extract
- ⅓ cup coconut oil
- ⅓ cup dark chocolate chips
- 1 batch homemade Caramel Sauce (see recipe below)

1. Preheat the oven to 350 F.
2. Mix the flour, powder, sugar, salt and baking soda in one bowl; mix the eggs, honey, vanilla and coconut oil in a second bowl.
3. Combine both mixtures and stir until all ingredients are incorporated together.
4. Pour the mixture into a greased 8 x 8 pan.
5. Top with the chocolate chips (and/or nuts, if desired), and bake for 25–30 minutes.
6. Let cool and then drizzle with the Caramel Sauce.

CARAMEL SAUCE

Serving Size: 6   Time: 25 minutes

- One 14-ounce can full-fat coconut milk
- ¾ cup coconut sugar
- ¼ cup raw honey
- 1 tablespoon coconut oil
- 1 teaspoon vanilla extract
- ½ teaspoon sea salt

1. Place the coconut milk, coconut sugar and honey in a saucepan. Bring to a boil and then reduce the heat and allow to simmer for 15 minutes.
2. Add in the coconut oil, vanilla and salt and mix. Place in the fridge and allow the mixture to cool completely before serving.

Crust:

- 3 cups walnuts
- 2 cups Medjool dates, pitted
- 1 teaspoon vanilla
- Dash of sea salt
  (about 1/6 teaspoon)

Filling:

- 1½ cups raw cashews,
  soaked and rinsed well*
- ⅓ cup maple syrup
- ½ teaspoon vanilla
- One 14-ounce can full-fat
  coconut milk
- ¼ cup lemon juice
- ⅓ cup dutch-processed
  cocoa powder
- ⅓ cup coconut oil, melted
- ½ teaspoon sea salt
- 1½ cup coconut flakes

COCONUT COCOA CHEESECAKE

Serving Size: 8–10   Time: 3 hours 5 minutes

---

*Quick soaked cashews: To cut down on soaking time, add the cashews to a pot and cover with water by $\frac{1}{2}$ inch. Bring to a boil and boil for 2 minutes. Remove from the heat and allow the cashews to soak for 1 hour. Drain the cashews, rinse with cold water and use.

1. Blend together the walnuts, dates, vanilla and salt in a food processor until the dough is formed.
2. Spread the dough evenly in the bottom of an ungreased 9-inch springform pan.
3. Place the pan in the freezer for 30 minutes.
4. Place all of the filling ingredients into a blender and blend on low speed until well combined.
5. Remove the crust from the freezer.
6. Pour the filling mixture on top of the crust, cover the pan and replace the cake in the freezer.
7. Freeze for at least 2 hours.
8. Defrost the cake in the refrigerator for 20 minutes before serving.
9. Sprinkle the coconut flakes on the top before serving.

Coconut Whipped Cream

COCONUT WHIPPED CREAM

Serving Size: 2   Time: Overnight

- **One 14-ounce can full-fat coconut milk**
- **1 teaspoon vanilla extract**
- **Liquid stevia or maple syrup to taste**

1. Allow the can of coconut milk to sit in the fridge overnight, untouched.
2. In the morning, open the can and scoop out the solid cream on top. Place the cream in a small mixing bowl. Pour the liquid into a different container.
3. Add the vanilla and stevia or syrup to taste and use a high-speed hand blender to whip the cream into soft peaks. Serve immediately.

COCONUT MILK PUDDING

Serving Size: 2   Time: 45 minutes

- **One 14-ounce can full fat coconut milk**
- **4 tablespoons raw honey**
- **2 tablespoons arrowroot powder**
- **2 eggs**
- **1 tablespoon vanilla extract**
- **2 tablespoons coconut oil**

1. Add the coconut milk and honey to a small pot over medium heat and bring to a boil. Reduce the heat and allow the mixture to cool.
2. In a separate bowl, whisk the arrowroot powder and eggs.
3. Slowly pour 1 cup of the coconut milk into the egg mixture, whisking constantly to prevent clumping.
4. Turn the heat setting of the coconut milk to low and slowly add the egg mixture, whisking constantly.
5. Once it thickens, remove from the heat and add in the vanilla and coconut oil.
6. Pour the contents into a bowl and allow to cool in the fridge for 30 minutes to 1 hour.

RASPBERRY CHOCOLATE CREPES

Serving Size: 6   Time: 30 minutes

Crepes:
- ½ cup cooked quinoa
- 2 tablespoons coconut oil
- 1 tablespoon cacao powder
- 4 tablespoons raw honey
- 6 eggs, well beaten
- 1 cup coconut flour
- ½ teaspoon each: sea salt, cinnamon and vanilla extract
- ½ cup full-fat coconut milk
- ⅓ cup water
- 1 cup red raspberries

Chocolate Sauce:
- ½ cup raw honey
- ½ cup cacao powder
- 2 tablespoons coconut oil, melted
- 1 teaspoon vanilla extract

1. Prepare the Coconut Whipped Cream (see page 179).
2. For crepes, mix all ingredients together (except for the raspberries) in a medium bowl. The batter should be very thin.
3. Place a small skillet over the heat with coconut oil. When skillet is warm, pour a cup of the batter into the skillet. Carefully flip the crepe and cook the other side until the consistency is no longer wet.
4. For chocolate sauce, blend all ingredients together in a food processor.
5. Put one crepe on a dessert plate, fill with a few crushed raspberries and fold the crepe in half. Add a dollop of the Coconut Whipped Cream and drizzle with the chocolate sauce.

SALTED CARAMEL CHOCOLATE CUPCAKES

Serving Size: 12   Time: 35 minutes

Cupcakes:
- ⅔ cup full-fat goat milk yogurt
- 2 teaspoons baking powder
- ½ teaspoon sea salt
- 2 eggs
- 1 tablespoon vanilla extract
- 1 cup unsalted grass-fed butter, softened
- 1 cup water
- 2 cups coconut sugar
- 2 cups almond flour
- 1 batch Caramel Sauce (see page 175)
- Sea salt for garnish

Cream Cheese Frosting:
- Two 8-ounce packages organic cream cheese
- 1 tablespoon vanilla extract
- 8 tablespoons unsalted grass-fed butter (1 stick), softened
- 3½ cups coconut sugar

1. Preheat the oven to 350 F. Line a cupcake tin with liners.
2. Whisk together the yogurt, baking soda, salt, eggs and vanilla in a small bowl.
3. Mix the butter and water in a larger bowl. Add the yogurt mixture and mix well.
4. Add the coconut sugar, almond flour and Caramel Sauce and mix well.
5. Fill the liners and bake for 18–25 minutes. Allow the cupcakes to cool.
6. To make the cream cheese frosting, beat together the cream cheese, vanilla, butter and sugar in a mixing bowl until soft and fluffy, starting on low speed and increasing to medium-high.

AVOCADO CHOCOLATE MOUSSE

Serving Size: 8–12   Time: 5–10 minutes

- ½ cup Medjool dates, pitted and soaked
- ½ cup maple syrup
- 1 teaspoon vanilla extract
- 1–1½ cups mashed avocado (2–3 avocados)
- ¾ cup raw cacao powder
- ½ cup water

1. Blend or process the dates, maple syrup and vanilla extract in a food processor until smooth. Add the mashed avocado and cacao powder and process until creamy, stopping to scrape down the sides of the bowl with a spatula if needed.
2. Add the water and process until smooth. Serve at room temperature or chilled. Store in a sealed container in the fridge up to 3 days or in the freezer up to 2 weeks.
3. For fudgesicles, freeze the mousse in ice cube trays. Thaw for 5 minutes before serving.
4. For chocolate sauce, increase water to 1 cup.

CASHEW BUTTER FUDGE

Serving Size: 8   Time: 2 hours

- **12 ounces cashew butter**
- **2 tablespoons coconut oil, melted**
- **2 tablespoons raw honey**
- **¼ teaspoon cinnamon**
- **⅛ teaspoon Himalayan salt**

1. Line an 8 x 8 baking with parchment paper and set aside.
2. Place all of the ingredients in a large bowl and use a hand mixer to thoroughly combine.
3. Pour the batter into the pan and freeze for a minimum of 2 hours.
4. Slice the fudge into squares and place into an airtight container and store in the freezer.
5. Keep the fudge frozen and pull out squares as a treat when needed.

NO-BAKE CASHEW TRUFFLES

Serving Size: 6–8   Time: 10 minutes

- 1 cup cashews
- 2 tablespoons cashew butter
- 6 Medjool dates, pitted
- ½ teaspoon cinnamon
- 1 teaspoon vanilla extract
- 3 tablespoons coconut oil, melted then cooled
- 1 tablespoon each: full-fat coconut milk and bone broth protein powder
- 1 teaspoon each: cinnamon and cocoa powder

1. Process the cashews until small chunks are formed. Add the cashew butter, dates, cinnamon, vanilla, oil, milk and bone broth powder, blending until the mixture becomes pasty.
2. Using your hands, roll the dough into bite-sized balls.
3. Dust with the cinnamon and cocoa powder mixture. Place in the fridge until firm, approximately 1 hour.

Coconut Boosters

COCONUT BOOSTERS

Serving Size: 4   Time: 1 hour 5 minutes

- **1 cup coconut oil**
- **½ cup chia seeds**
- **1 teaspoon vanilla extract**
- **1 tablespoon raw honey**

1. Mix all ingredients together in a bowl.
2. Spoon into candy molds and freeze for an hour.

DARK CHOCOLATE ALMOND BUTTER COOKIES

Serving Size: 12   Time: 20 minutes

- **1 cup sprouted almond butter**
- **½ cup almond flour**
- **⅓ cup maple syrup**
- **1 egg**
- **1 tablespoon vanilla extract**
- **½ teaspoon each: sea salt, baking soda and baking powder**
- **½ cup dark chocolate bar, minimum 72% cacao, broken into pieces**

1. Preheat the oven to 350 F.
2. Place all ingredients in a food processor and process until smooth.
3. Chill the dough for 20 minutes.
4. Roll 2 tablespoons of dough into balls and place on parchment paper-lined baking sheet.
5. Bake for 10 minutes.

DARK CHOCOLATE CAKE

Serving Size: 8   Time: 45 minutes

- 2 cups coconut flour
- 2 cups coconut sugar
- ¾ cup cacao powder
- 2 teaspoons baking powder
- 1½ teaspoons baking soda
- 1 teaspoon sea salt
- 1 cup full-fat coconut milk
- ½ cup coconut oil
- 6 eggs
- 1 tablespoon vanilla extract
- 1 cup organic coffee
- 2 batches Caramel Sauce (see page 178)

1. Preheat the oven to 350 F.
2. Grease and flour two 9-inch cake pans.
3. Mix the flour, sugar, cacao powder, baking powder, baking soda and salt in a bowl.
4. Add the coconut milk, oil, eggs and vanilla and mix until combined.
5. Carefully add the coffee and mix until fluffy.
6. Distribute the batter evenly between the cake pans and bake for 30–35 minutes, or until cooked through.
7. Allow to cook through. Remove from the oven and allow to cool completely before removing from the cake pans.
8. Spread one cooled batch of Caramel Sauce evenly over one cake and then stack the other. Cover with the second batch of Caramel Sauce and serve.

COCONUT MACAROONS

Serving Size: 48 macaroons   **Time: 20 minutes**

- **6 egg whites**
- **¼ teaspoon sea salt**
- **½ cup raw honey**
- **1 tablespoon vanilla extract**
- **3 cups coconut flakes**

1. Whisk the eggs and salt in a mixing bowl until peaks form in the eggs.
2. Add in the honey, vanilla and coconut flakes.
3. Drop the batter onto parchment paper on a cookie sheet.
4. Pinch off each at the top like a chocolate kiss.
5. Bake at 350 F for 10–15 minutes, or until lightly browned.

Special Thanks

First, I want to thank God, my lord and savior Jesus Christ, for loving me and giving me the opportunity, the influence and the gifts to create this cookbook.

To my wife Chelsea, you are the light of my life, and I couldn't have ever written a cookbook without your profound influence. Your wisdom and love make me a better man, leader and teacher.

To my editor Ethan Boldt, whose strategizing and final touches always help make the finished product a masterpiece.

To my designer Allison Brochey, whose expertise and hard work not only helped this cookbook look as good as it does, but also all that we do at DrAxe.com.

To Ayla Sadler, for helping me develop a book full of easy-to-follow, delicious and healing recipes for the gut — and which will hopefully help millions of people live longer, healthier lives.

To the DrAxe.com team, including Evan, Mike, Joe, Lora and Mary, I could not do this alone. It takes not only a team, but a passionate group of A players to change the world.

To my parents Winona and Gary Axe, thank you for raising me in a loving home and always encouraging me. Mom, you are the most courageous person I know and taught me the importance of prayer and persistence. Dad, you taught me discipline, humility and the importance of doing plenty of pull-ups.

To my in-laws Sherri and Joel Vreeman, thank you for all of your love and support, and for being an example of how to be a light in the world.

To Axe Nation and the Axe Ambassadors, thank you for passionately helping spread this message of health and natural healing.

Recipe Index

Notes

Dr. Josh Axe, DNM, DC, CNS, is a bestselling author, certified doctor of natural medicine, doctor of chiropractic, clinical nutritionist, and founder of one of the top 5 natural health websites in the world, with more than 10 million readers per month. Dr. Axe is the author of the books *Eat Dirt* and *Essential Oils: Ancient Medicine for a Modern World*, and he's the co-founder of Ancient Nutrition and Axe Organics.

For more helpful resources, visit www.DrAxe.com. It's the home for natural remedies, healthy recipes, nutrition and fitness advice, essential oils and natural supplements.

www.DrAxe.com